200 recipes

200 recipes for kids

hamlyn **all color**

Emma Jane Frost

An Hachette UK Company
www.hachette.co.uk

First published in Great Britain in 2009 by Hamlyn,
a division of Octopus Publishing Group Ltd
2–4 Heron Quays, London E14 4JP
www.octopusbooksusa.com

Distributed in the U.S. and Canada by Octopus Books USA:
c/o Hachette Book Group
237 Park Avenue
New York NY 10017

Some of the recipes in this book have previously
appeared in other books published by Hamlyn.

ISBN: 978-0-600-62089-1

Printed and bound in China

1 2 3 4 5 6 7 8 9 10

Standard level spoon measurements are used in all recipes.

Ovens should be preheated to the specified temperature
—if using a fan-assisted oven, follow the manufacturer's
instructions for adjusting the time and the temperature.

Fresh herbs should be used unless otherwise stated.

Medium eggs should be used unless otherwise stated.

Portion sizes are for the average adult and child aged
around seven, so you will need to adjust portions
according to the appetite and age of your child.

contents

introduction

introduction

In our minds, mealtimes are a relaxing and happy affair. Children and parents eat together around the table, conversation is exchanged, and every plate is scraped clean. The reality of feeding a family is usually very different. There is often only one parent in the kitchen trying to keep the children entertained while preparing the meal, the main ingredient is often in the freezer when it should have been defrosted at least 24 hours previously, and one child needs to get to a swimming lesson! Because we would all love a more stress-free life, this book has been written to help make mealtimes less of a battle, more fun, more interesting—not to mention healthier and more successful for everybody involved.

Recipes for every occasion

As parents, we all know that children can be notoriously difficult to cook for. Many of us fall into the habit of cooking the same dishes over and over, simply because we cannot bear the idea of scraping wasted food into the garbage at the end of a meal. However, a child's formative years are when they learn to accept and like new foods, and it is therefore of great importance to encourage them to experiment with new tastes and different textures as often as you can.

This book has been put together with this in mind, but also with the knowledge that children are generally fussy creatures and like their food to be simple and to look good. Each recipe has been photographed to show you exactly what you will be cooking (and what they will be eating), and has of course been tested for child-appeal. To prevent your children getting bored by the same meals, we have also added a creative variation at the end of each recipe, giving you all the mealtime inspiration you should ever need for your family in one handy package!

Breakfast time

The first chapter gives you no fewer than 22 ideas for new breakfasts. Most children start the day with a bowl of store-bought cereal, but remember that children's

metabolism is very high. Particularly for those children who are going to school, breakfast really is the most important meal of the day, in that it is designed to power them all the way through to lunchtime. A hungry stomach will lead to lack of concentration, and a lack of nutrients does not bode well for a good brain function, so fill them up in the morning with great food that they will love—fruit, seeds, oats, eggs, and yogurt—and see what a difference it makes to their day.

Lunchtime

The next chapter, "Inspired lunches," is designed to break you out of the cheese, tuna, and ham sandwich rut that so many of us find ourselves in at lunchtime. Toddlers and youngsters of preschool age are very often extremely hungry by midday, and a filling and nutritious meal is vital to ward off the grizzles later in the day.

Dinnertime

The "Delicious dinners" you will find in the next chapter are exactly that—tried and trusted meals that kids will always eat and you will love. Some of these recipes may involve a little more work than others, but they have been included because they go down well with nearly every child around the table. They are therefore a great choice not just for your own children but also for when you have visitors for tea and you need to cater for varying tastes. And remember, if your children eat well at dinnertime, bedtime will inevitably be a calmer and happier experience.

Portable meals

Eating meals in the car on the way back from sport training, or in the buggy on the way to pick up siblings from school, is unfortunately systematic of today's busy lifestyles. The "On-the-run suppers" chapter is designed to take some of the stress out of those particularly busy days when a meal around the dining table really is impossible. The theory is that these recipes should be portable and fairly mess-free to eat in the car, buggy, or the leisure center, but do remember your kitchen foil, plastic wrap, and baby wipes because spillages will undoubtedly occur.

Eating out

The chapter called "Café alternatives" has been included because, like adults, most children like the idea of being treated to a meal out. These ideas are for when the budget does not stretch to a real café meal or for when time (or toddlers) don't allow for painful waits in understaffed restaurants. If you have the time and inclination, you can make these meals even more fun by setting the table in a different room, on a rug on the floor, or outside in the garden to give everybody a change from the norm. Better still, keep in stock a selection of cardboard, party-size, fold-out lunchboxes and serve your "café" meal in these; you'll be surprised how much your child enjoys eating from a novelty container.

Nutritious snacks

"Snack," in some people's minds, is a dirty word. It conjures up images of additive-ridden candy bars and unnecessary, fattening treats. Actually, children invariably need nutritional snacks in between their three meals a day to keep their energy levels up and prevent attacks of bad behavior. You will find that a lot of the recipes in the "Super snacks" chapter are full of nutritious treats—vitamin-packed fruit, a selection of nuts and seeds (an excellent, portable form of protein), and an array of wholegrains to sustain energy.

Desserts

A sweet course is sometimes regarded as an old-fashioned concept and has connotations of being stodgy and tasteless, but there is always a time and a place for spoiling children with a home-cooked, filling, and nutritional dessert. Nearly all children love the taste of sugar, so when better to introduce them to new fruits and exotic tastes than with their dessert? Try the recipes in this chapter and watch your children wolf down raw and cooked fruit mixed in with crumble toppings, pancakes, chocolate, ice cream, and tasty homemade custard.

The time factor

Feeding children, whether aged 2 or 12, can take time, so all the recipes in this book have been written with speed and ease in mind. At first, the recipes may take a little longer to prepare than you expect, and, if you have got stuck in the "fish fingers and spaghetti bolognaise" rut, learning to use new ingredients will take a little time. The key to preparing successful meals for children is planning. This book provides a whole array of inspiring recipe ideas for breakfasts, lunches, dinners, and snacks, so do try to find a few minutes (difficult though it may seem with a house full of demanding children) to plan your week's meals, buying only what you need for the recipes and defrosting meat and fish in plenty of time.

It is more important than ever when cooking for children that you have the staples to hand in your pantry, so always ensure your kitchen is stocked with the key ingredients that make great children's meals—soy sauce, all-purpose flour, dried pasta shapes, cheddar and Parmesan cheese, chicken bouillon cubes, tomato paste, olive oil, coconut milk, cinnamon, nutmeg, and other herbs and spices. It is also wise to keep some nutrient-dense vegetables in the freezer to add into kids' meals—frozen spinach, corn, and peas are usually great favorites. Don't forget, either, to have a spare can of tomatoes and some cans of salmon or tuna always at hand to help you whiz up a last-minute wonder.

Getting children involved

It may seem a bit of a cliché, but getting your children involved in the preparation of their food will almost certainly help their acceptance of it at the dinner table. Helping to prepare the meal will bring food into a child's imagination, and they can start to see it as an exciting part of their day. For this reason, many of the recipes in this book have been written with your child's participation in mind, no matter what their age or ability.

For instance, the Asparagus in Blankets recipe on pages 58–59 is great for encouraging children to try asparagus for the first time. Encourage them to roll the spears in prosciutto and let them sprinkle the Parmesan cheese over the top—young children will love "peeping" the asparagus out through the tunnels. Alternatively, get them involved with chopping and sprinkling the ham and olives on top of the Mini Scone Pizzas on pages 118–119. Many children love watching the whizzing-up of the Breakfast Smoothies on pages 32–33—but beware, as the noise of the blender may make younger children run from the room.

Growing your own ingredients

Taking this concept a stage further, parents of children who refuse to eat fruit and vegetables could benefit from getting out in the yard and growing some easy garden produce. Growing carrots from seed in large plastic tubs, for example, is a hugely rewarding experience for a child, particularly when they get to dig up the carrots and crunch them with the green tops still on.

For those with good intentions but no outdoor space, simply sprouting seeds on a windowsill can offer great benefits to your child's diet. Sprouted seeds are packed full of nutrients, and most children will love growing them and then sprinkling them over pasta or baked potatoes. Growing herbs such as thyme, parsley, and mint in windowboxes is also a great way to get additional vitamins into your kids' meals—their job can be to pick the herbs, chop them, and stir them into their own meals. This gives them a sense of ownership over the meal and helps them to feel in control of their food.

Choosing ingredients

When you are buying the ingredients for the recipes in this book, try to buy the freshest ingredients you can—fruit and vegetables start to lose their nutrients the moment they are picked, so the quicker you eat them after picking the more beneficial they are for your child.

Depending on your budget, you may also consider using organic ingredients. More and more people are choosing organic foodstuffs for their family, and it is easy to see why. Organic food has more beneficial minerals, essential amino acids, and vitamins than non-organic food. Organic milk, for instance, has nearly 70% more essential fatty acid omega-3 than its non-organic equivalent. Organic meat is free from pesticides, chemicals, and antibiotics, and organic crops are grown naturally and not routinely sprayed with pesticides. Although many of these pesticides are probably harmless, scientific tests are still being done to discover if there are any lasting negative effects on our health; until we know the outcome, it is worth buying organic foods to benefit our children with the additional nutrients they contain.

Portions and eating together

Most of the recipes in this book have been worked out based on a family of four—two adults and two children aged around seven—eating together. Obviously, if you are only catering for yourself plus one or two youngsters, it may be wise to halve the ingredients or, if the recipe allows, cook the whole amount and freeze a couple of portions for another day.

Whenever possible, however, it is recommended that you take the time to sit and eat with your children, for two main reasons. First, you are a role model for your kids, so if they see you eating a new food they are more likely to try it themselves. Second, mealtimes should be a social occasion, a time to talk and laugh and generally catch up with the day's activities. With today's busy lifestyles—working parents, afterschool clubs and single parenting—it is rare for a parent to find the time to sit down and just talk with their children. Whenever possible, try to take time over a meal, particularly those meals where you are introducing new foods, and remember to praise a child who tries a new food, even if it is only a taste.

Get cooking!

A successful meal takes a bit of planning, a little time, some good ingredients, a dash of inspiration, and some gentle encouragement. If cooking for your children has to date been a disappointing experience, this book should provide you with plenty of inspiration to turn the tide on those mealtime battles.

breakfasts

hot peach & cinnamon pancakes

Makes **8**
Preparation time **10 minutes**
Cooking time **20 minutes**

3 small ripe **peaches**
1 teaspoon **ground cinnamon**
6 tablespoons **maple syrup**
1 cup **self-rising flour**
2 tablespoons **superfine sugar**
1 **egg**
⅔ cup **milk**
little **oil**, for greasing

Halve and pit the peaches. Roughly chop 1 of them and set it aside, then cut the remaining 2 into wedges and toss with a small pinch of the ground cinnamon and all the maple syrup in a small bowl and set aside.

Sift the flour and remaining cinnamon into a bowl and add the superfine sugar. Make a well in the center and set aside. Beat the egg and milk together well in a pitcher, then pour into the center of the flour mixture. Mix quickly and as lightly as possible to make a batter the consistency of thick cream. Stir in the chopped peaches.

Lightly oil a heavy skillet or flat griddle pan. Drop heaping tablespoons of the batter onto the pan surface and cook over a steady, moderate heat for 1–2 minutes until bubbles rise to the surface and burst. Turn the pancake over and cook for 1–2 minutes more. Remove from the pan and keep warm while making the remaining pancakes.

Serve the pancakes warm, with a large spoonful of the peach and maple syrup mixture over the top of each.

For creamy banana pancakes, make the batter as above, replacing the peaches with 1 small banana, roughly chopped. Cook for 1 minute on each side until golden, and serve with 1 thinly sliced banana tossed with 2 tablespoons maple syrup over the top.

toffee-apple oatmeal

Serves **4**
Preparation time **10 minutes**
Cooking time **15 minutes**

1 lb **dessert apples**, peeled,
  cored, and roughly chopped
½ teaspoon **ground mixed
  spice**
½ teaspoon **ground ginger**
5 tablespoons **brown sugar**
8 tablespoons **water**
2½ cups **milk**
1½ cups **rolled oats**

Place the apples in a medium, heavy saucepan
with the spices, 3 tablespoons of the sugar, and
the measured water. Bring to a boil, then reduce
the heat to a simmer. Cover and simmer over a very
gentle heat for 4–5 minutes, stirring occasionally,
until the apples are soft yet still retaining some of
their shape. Set aside with a lid to keep warm while
making the oatmeal.

Bring the milk and remaining sugar to a boil,
stirring occasionally. Remove from the heat and
add the rolled oats. Stir well, then return to a low
heat, stirring continuously for 4–5 minutes until the
oatmeal has thickened.

Stir half the apple mixture through the oatmeal until
well mixed, then ladle into 4 warmed serving bowls.
Spoon over the remaining apple mixture and drizzle
with the toffee apple syrup to serve, if desired.

For hot-pink, swirled oatmeal, mash 2 cups fresh
raspberries with 1 teaspoon superfine sugar. Make up
the oatmeal following the method above, then remove
from the heat and spoon in the mashed raspberries.
Using 1–2 stirs only, swirl the raspberries into the
oatmeal, then ladle the swirled oatmeal into warmed
bowls and serve with spoonfuls of thick yogurt on top,
if desired.

late great breakfast

Serves **4**
Preparation time **15 minutes**
Cooking time **15–20 minutes**

13 oz sheet ready-rolled **puff pastry**
1 **red bell pepper**, cored, seeded, and roughly chopped
2 **tomatoes**, cut into wedges
4 oz **button mushrooms**, cut in half
2 tablespoons **olive oil**
6 **eggs**
8 thin-cut slices **bacon**
1 tablespoon **butter**, plus extra for greasing

Unroll the pastry and cut out four 5 x 4 inch rectangles. Using the tip of a small knife, make a shallow cut about ½ inch in from the edges of each rectangle, making sure you don't cut right through to the base. Place the pastry rectangles on a greased baking sheet.

Arrange the bell pepper, tomatoes, and mushrooms on the pastry rectangles, keeping them away from the marked rims. Drizzle with 1 tablespoon of the oil and bake in a preheated oven, 425°F, for 15–20 minutes until the pastry is well risen and golden.

While the pastry shells are baking, beat the eggs in a bowl. Heat the remaining oil in a skillet and gently fry the bacon for about 2 minutes on each side until crisp, turning the slices with a turner or wooden spatula. Melt the butter in a large saucepan. Tip in the beaten eggs and cook over a gentle heat, stirring continuously until scrambled.

Remove the baking sheet from the oven and transfer the pastries to serving plates. Spoon some scrambled eggs onto the center of each and top with the bacon slices. Serve while still hot.

For sausage & tomato pasties, place 8 good-quality chipolata sausages under a hot broiler and cook, turning, for 8–10 minutes until golden and cooked, adding 8 halved, small tomatoes to the broiler pan cut side up for the final 5 minutes of cooking. Halve the sausages and toss with the tomatoes and 1 tablespoon chopped parsley and use to fill the pastries, as above.

french toast with blueberries

Serves **4**
Preparation time **5 minutes**
Cooking time **10 minutes**

2 **eggs**
2 tablespoons **superfine
  sugar**
½ teaspoon **ground cinnamon**
4 tablespoons **milk**
2 tablespoons **butter**
4 thick slices **brioche**
1 cup **blueberries**
8 tablespoons thick **yogurt**
4 teaspoons **honey**, to drizzle

Beat the eggs in a bowl with the sugar, cinnamon, and
milk. Heat the butter in a large, heavy skillet. Dip the
brioche slices, 2 at a time, into the egg mixture on both
sides, then lift into the hot pan and fry for 1−2 minutes
on each side until golden.

Repeat with the remaining brioche slices. Mix half the
blueberries into the yogurt.

Serve the warm French toasts with spoonfuls of the
yogurt on top, the remaining blueberries sprinkled over,
and a thin drizzle of honey on top.

For sugar & cinnamon French toast, make the
French toasts as above and place on serving plates
once cooked and warm. Mix ¼ cup Demerara sugar
with ½ teaspoon ground cinnamon. Dredge each
of the warm French toasts with the cinnamon sugar
and serve.

herby beans & bacon

Serves **4**
Preparation time **10 minutes**
Cooking time **15 minutes**

1 tablespoon **olive oil**
6 **bacon** slices, thickly
  chopped
1 small **carrot**, finely grated
13 oz can **chopped tomatoes**
3 tablespoons **tomato paste**
2 tablespoons **honey**
13 oz can **cranberry beans**,
  drained and rinsed
3 tablespoons chopped **flat-
  leaf parsley** (optional)
4 thick slices **whole-wheat** or
  multigrain bread
¼ cup freshly grated
  Parmesan cheese (optional)

Heat the oil in a large, heavy skillet, then cook the bacon over a moderate heat for 2–3 minutes until beginning to turn pale golden. Add the carrot and cook for 1 minute more.

Add the tomatoes, tomato paste, and honey and heat until the tomato juice is bubbling. Add the beans, then reduce the heat and simmer for 4 minutes, uncovered, until the tomato juice has reduced and thickened slightly. Stir in the parsley, if desired, and set aside.

Lightly toast the bread under a broiler until golden and just crisp. Place on warmed serving plates and pile the herby beans and bacon on top. Sprinkle with the Parmesan, if desired.

For sausage & beans, cook 4 good-quality sausages in the oil for 5–6 minutes, turning until golden. Remove from the pan and slice, then return to the pan with 4 oz thinly sliced chorizo sausage and cook for 2 minutes, stirring occasionally until the sausages are golden. Continue as above and serve sprinkled with Parmesan, if desired.

morning muffins & tomato ketchup

Serves **4**
Preparation time **15 minutes**
Cooking time **20–25 minutes**

1 lb good-quality **sausages**
1 tablespoon chopped
  rosemary
3 tablespoons chopped
  parsley
1 tablespoon **honey**
1 teaspoon **vinegar**
4 **eggs**
2 **English muffins**, halved

Ketchup
13 oz can **chopped tomatoes**
2 tablespoons **maple syrup**
1 tablespoon **brown sugar**
3 tablespoons **red wine**
  vinegar

Place all the ketchup ingredients into a small, heavy skillet and bring to a boil. Reduce the heat and gently simmer for 5–7 minutes, uncovered, stirring occasionally until the sauce is thick and pulpy. Whiz in a food processor until smooth, then place in a jar and cool. (Store in a refrigerator for up to 2 weeks.)

Cut along the length of each sausage, ease the skin off and discard it. Place the sausagemeat in a bowl with the herbs and honey and mix well. Using damp hands, shape into 8 small patties, then cook under a preheated medium broiler for 10–12 minutes, turning once, until golden.

Meanwhile, bring a skillet half-filled with water, with the vinegar added, to a boil. Reduce the heat to a simmer, then immediately break the eggs, well spaced apart, into the water and cook for 1 minute until the white is opaque. Remove from the water using a slotted spoon and keep warm.

Toast the muffin halves until golden and lightly crisp. Place a warm muffin half onto each of 4 serving plates and top with 2 sausage patties, a poached egg, and a spoonful of ketchup.

For tomato & mushroom muffins, heat 1 tablespoon olive oil in a heavy skillet and cook 8 oz halved chestnut mushrooms and 4 halved plum tomatoes over a moderate heat for 4–5 minutes until soft and golden, turning occasionally. Poach the eggs and toast the muffins as above. Serve the muffins with the warm tomatoes, mushrooms, and eggs on top with a drizzle of ketchup.

crunchy honey yogurt

Serves **6**
Preparation time **10 minutes**
Cooking time **5 minutes**

2 cups **Greek** or **whole milk
yogurt**
¾ cup **strawberries**, quartered

Topping
½ cup **slivered almonds**
½ cup **pumpkin seeds**
½ cup **sunflower seeds**
3 tablespoons **sesame seeds**
½ cup **rolled oats**
6 tablespoons **superfine
sugar**
4 tablespoons **honey**, plus
extra to drizzle (optional)

Mix the almonds, seeds, oats, and sugar in a
large bowl. Line a large baking sheet with nonstick
parchment paper, then pour the nut and seed mixture
over. Lightly shake the baking sheet to level the
ingredients.

Drizzle the honey in thin streams over the top,
then place under a preheated medium broiler for
3–4 minutes until the sugar begins to caramelize and
the nuts and seeds turn golden brown. Remove from
the broiler and set aside to cool and harden. Place the
hardened nuts and seeds in a plastic bag and bash
with a rolling pin to crush into a crunchy topping.

Spoon the yogurt into a bowl and fold in the
strawberries. Divide between 6 serving bowls and
sprinkle with the topping. (Store any leftover topping
in an airtight container for up to 2 weeks.) Drizzle with
more honey, if desired.

For yogurt-coated cereal topping, melt 4 oz white
chocolate in a heatproof bowl set over a pan of gently
simmering water. Remove from the heat and add
2 tablespoons of plain yogurt. Crunch up 2 cups
cornflakes and 2 whole shredded wheat biscuits onto
a parchment-paper-lined baking sheet and sprinkle
with ¾ cup rice puffs. Drizzle over the warm white
chocolate and yogurt coating and refrigerate for
1 hour until set. Once set, transfer the paper to a
cutting board and roughly chop the cereals to form
a rough and chunky topping.

banana & choc whole-wheat muffins

Makes **12**
Preparation time **15 minutes**
Cooking time **20–25 minutes**

1 cup **self-rising whole-wheat flour**
1¼ cups **all-purpose flour**
1 teaspoon **baking powder**
1 teaspoon **baking soda**
½ teaspoon **salt**
½ cup **superfine sugar**
3 large ripe **bananas**, mashed
1 **egg**, beaten
5 tablespoons **water**
5 tablespoons **vegetable oil**
3 oz **carob** or **semisweet chocolate**, roughly chopped

Sift the flours, baking powder, baking soda, and salt into a large bowl, then add the wheatgerm left in the sifter. Stir in the superfine sugar. Mix together the bananas, egg, measured water, and oil in a pitcher, then pour into the dry ingredients and gently mix until just combined. Fold in the carob or chocolate.

Line a 12-cup muffin pan with 12 paper muffin cups and three-quarters fill each with the mixture.

Bake in a preheated oven, 350°F, for 20–25 minutes until they are well risen and spring back when you press them. Place on a wire rack to cool.

For fresh cherry & vanilla muffins, omit the bananas, mix 2 teaspoons vanilla extract into the egg, water, and oil mixture, and fold in 1 cup fresh pitted cherries instead of the chocolate. Bake as above.

breakfast smoothies

Serves **2**
Preparation time **5 minutes**

2 bananas
1¼ cups **milk**
4 tablespoons plain **yogurt**
3 tablespoons **maple syrup**
½ cup **instant oats**

To serve
banana slices
malt loaf, cut into chunks

Place the bananas in a food processor with the milk, yogurt, and maple syrup and blend until smooth. Add the instant oats and whiz again to thicken. Pour into 2 large glasses.

Arrange banana slices and chunks of malt loaf on 2 toothpicks and balance them across the top of the glasses, to serve.

For peanut-butter smoothies, replace the bananas with 4 tablespoons crunchy peanut butter, and change the maple syrup to honey. Make as above, whizzing until smooth.

breakfast crumble

Serves **8**

Preparation time **30 minutes**

Cooking time **45–50 minutes**

1 lb **dessert apples**, peeled, cored, and roughly chopped

8 oz **pears**, peeled, cored, and roughly chopped

finely grated zest and juice of **1 orange**

4 tablespoons **honey**

½ teaspoon **ground ginger**

1 cup **strawberries**, hulled and quartered

Crumble

½ cup **all-purpose flour**

3 tablespoons **cold-milled flax seed (ground linseed)**

¼ cup **butter**, cubed

½ cup **rolled oats**

½ cup **mixed seeds** (such as pumpkin, sunflower, sesame, and hemp)

⅓ cup **Demerara sugar**

Place the apples and pears in a medium, heavy saucepan with the orange zest and juice, honey, and ginger. Bring to a gentle simmer, stirring occasionally, then cover and simmer for 10 minutes until soft and slightly pulpy. Add the strawberries and cook for an additional 2–3 minutes until soft, yet still retaining their shape. Remove the pan from the heat and transfer the mixture to an ovenproof gratin dish. Set aside while making the crumble.

Put the flour in a bowl and stir in the flax seed. Add the butter and blend into the mixture until it resembles chunky bread crumbs. Add the oats and again blend the fat into the mixture using your fingertips to distribute well. Stir in the seeds and sugar then sprinkle over the fruit.

Bake in a preheated oven, 400°F, for 30–35 minutes until the topping is golden. Serve the crumble warm.

For amber crumble, omit the apples, pears, and strawberries, roughly chop 4 ripe peaches and 6 ripe apricots and segment 4 oranges, then toss with 4 tablespoons honey and 1 teaspoon ground cinnamon. Place the uncooked fruit in the gratin dish, sprinkle with the crumble, and bake as above.

melting mushrooms

Serves **4**
Preparation time **10 minutes**
Cooking time **9–12 minutes**

2 tablespoon **olive oil**
4 large flat **mushrooms**
4 small fresh **tomatoes**,
   roughly chopped
1 tablespoon **tomato paste**
4 tablespoons canned
   cannellini beans, drained
   and rinsed
1 tablespoon **honey**
1 tablespoon chopped **parsley**
2 oz **Gruyère** or **Edam
   cheese**, thinly sliced
1 tablespoon freshly grated
   Parmesan cheese
4 slices **whole-wheat toast**,
   to serve

Heat the oil in a large, heavy skillet and cook the mushrooms over a moderate heat for 2–3 minutes, turning once, until they are softened. Place the mushrooms, stalk side up, on a foil-lined broiler rack.

Add the tomatoes to the pan juices, and cook, stirring occasionally, for 4–5 minutes until the tomatoes are thick and pulpy. Add the tomato paste, beans, and honey and continue to cook for 1 minute more. Remove from the heat and stir in the parsley.

Divide the mixture between the mushrooms and arrange the slices of Gruyère or Edam over the top. Sprinkle the mushrooms with the Parmesan and place under a preheated hot broiler for 2–3 minutes until golden and bubbling. Serve with slices of hot buttered whole-wheat toast.

For egg-topped melting mushrooms, follow the recipe as above. Toward the end, poach 4 eggs in a skillet half-filled with boiling water with 1 teaspoon vinegar for 1–2 minutes, then remove from the water using a slotted spoon and place on the mushrooms.

inspired lunches

traffic-light scrambled eggs

Serves **4**

Preparation time **10 minutes**

Cooking time **10 minutes**

3 tablespoons **olive oil**

1 small **onion**, finely chopped

½ **green bell pepper**, cored, seeded, and roughly chopped

½ **red bell pepper**, cored, seeded, and roughly chopped

½ **yellow bell pepper**, cored, seeded, and roughly chopped

1 **garlic** clove, crushed

3 tablespoons **water**

6 **eggs**, beaten

6 tablespoons **light cream**

4 thick slices **whole-wheat bread**, to serve

Heat the oil in a large, nonstick skillet and cook the onion and peppers over a moderate heat for about 4–5 minutes until softened. Add the garlic and cook for 1 minute more, then add the measured water. Cover the pan and simmer for 2 minutes.

Beat together the eggs and cream in a pitcher. Remove the lid from the pan, pour in the eggs, and stir over a low heat with a wooden spoon until the eggs are creamy and cooked.

Meanwhile, lightly toast the bread slices. Serve the eggs spooned over the warm toast.

For cheesy eggs & cress, beat together the eggs, cream, and ½ cup grated cheddar cheese in a pitcher. Heat 1 tablespoon butter in a large nonstick skillet and add the egg mixture. Stir over a low heat with a wooden spoon until creamy and cooked. Serve on warm whole-wheat toast with freshly cut cress sprinkled over.

hummus pita pockets

Serves **6**

Preparation time **15 minutes**

Cooking time **3 minutes**

13 oz can **chickpeas**, drained
and rinsed

3 tablespoons **tahini paste**

finely grated zest and juice
of ½ **lemon**

1 tablespoon **olive oil**

3 tablespoons chopped
chives (optional)

4 tablespoons **water**

2 medium **carrots**, grated

½ **cucumber**, chopped

handful of freshly cut **cress**

4 whole-wheat or white **pita
breads**

Place the chickpeas in a food processor with the tahini
paste and whiz until thick. Add the lemon zest and
juice, olive oil, chives, and measured water. Whiz again
until smooth and creamy.

Toss the carrots, cucumber, and cress in a bowl.

Lightly toast the pita breads for 1 minute until warm
and slightly "puffed." Halve each pita and fill, while
warm, with the hummus and salad. Serve immediately.

For pockets with beet hummus, place 6 oz cooked,
drained beets (not in vinegar) into a food processor
with 2 tablespoons tahini paste, the juice of ½ lemon,
and 1 teaspoon horseradish sauce. Whiz until smooth
and creamy. Use to fill the pita pockets as above, with
the salad.

jeweled couscous

Serves **2–3**

Preparation time **20 minutes**

Cooking time **2 minutes**

¾ cup **couscous**

⅔ cup hot **vegetable stock**

2 oz **green beans**, trimmed
and cut into ½ inch lengths

1 small **orange**

2 tablespoons **olive oil**

1 tablespoon **honey**

1 **pomegranate**

½ small **pineapple**, chopped
into small pieces

1 small **red bell pepper**, cored,
seeded, and finely diced

Put the couscous in a heatproof bowl and add the stock. Cover and allow to stand for 20 minutes.

Meanwhile, bring a small pan of water to a boil and add the beans. Cook for 2 minutes. Drain the beans through a colander and rinse in cold water.

Finely grate half the zest of the orange and mix it in a small bowl with 3 tablespoons of orange juice, the oil, and the honey. Beat lightly with a fork.

Cut the pomegranate in half. Pull the fruit apart with your hands and ease out the clusters of seeds. Separate the seeds, discarding any white parts of the fruit, which are bitter. Add the pomegranate seeds, beans, pineapple, and bell pepper to the couscous along with the orange and honey dressing. Mix well and chill in the refrigerator until ready to serve.

For chicken, pea, & mint couscous, make the couscous as above and allow to stand. Replace all the above vegetables with 6 oz cooked chicken, 1 cup cooked peas, and 3 tablespoons fresh chopped mint. Mix the zest and juice of half a lemon into ¾ cup plain yogurt and serve spooned over the couscous.

cheesy red dip with breadsticks

Serves **4**

Preparation time **45 minutes**, plus resting

Cooking time **30–40 minutes**

4 cups **all-purpose flour**

½ teaspoon **salt**

1 teaspoon **sugar**

¼ oz instant **dried yeast**

1¼ cups **warm water**

6 tablespoons **olive oil**

2 tablespoons **sesame seeds**

1 tablespoon **poppy seeds**

Dip

2 **red bell peppers**, cored, seeded, and quartered

2 **tomatoes**

1 tablespoon **olive oil**

1 tablespoon **balsamic vinegar**

¾ cup **cream cheese**

1 tablespoon chopped **thyme** (optional)

Sift the flour and salt into a large bowl and add the sugar and yeast. Stir in the measured warm water and 3 tablespoons of the oil. Mix well to form a smooth dough, then turn out onto a well-floured surface and knead for 10 minutes until smooth and elastic. Cover and allow to rest for 15 minutes before kneading again for 10 minutes more. Return to the bowl, cover with plastic wrap, and allow to stand for 30 minutes.

Knead the dough again to knock out the air, then cut into 4 pieces. Cut each quarter into 4 pieces, then stretch and roll each piece to make a long breadstick shape. Brush a baking sheet with the remaining oil. Roll the breadsticks in the oil, then sprinkle half with the sesame seeds and half with the poppy seeds. Bake in a preheated oven, 350°F, for 30 minutes until golden and crisp. Remove from the oven and allow to cool.

Meanwhile, place the bell peppers on a baking sheet with the tomatoes and drizzle with the oil. Roast for 30 minutes in the oven with the breadsticks. Remove and place in a plastic bag and allow to cool. Remove from the bag and peel away the skins and discard. Place in a food processor with all the cooking juices, vinegar, cheese, and thyme, if using, and whiz until well blended and rough-textured. Transfer to a serving bowl and serve with the breadsticks.

For creamy avocado dip, place 1 large quartered avocado in a food processor with the finely grated zest and juice of 1 lime, 6 tablespoons cream cheese, and 2 tablespoons sweet chili sauce and whiz until smooth. Serve with the breadsticks.

beef & asparagus bagels

Serves **2**

Preparation time **5 minutes**

Cooking time **2 minutes**

4 **asparagus spears**, each
  cut into three
1 cup **watercress**
1 tablespoon **low-fat
  mayonnaise**
1 teaspoon **Dijon mustard**
  (optional)
2 **multigrain bagels**
4 oz **cooked beef**, very thinly
  sliced

Put a pan of lightly salted water on to boil. Boil the asparagus, if fresh, briefly, for 30 seconds or so, then drain well and set aside. (Asparagus in jars does not need cooking.)

Remove the larger stalks from the watercress and chop it. Place the mayonnaise and mustard, if using, in a bowl and stir in the watercress.

Split the bagels in half and toast under a preheated broiler. Spread the halves with the flavored mayonnaise. Top with the beef and asparagus spears and wrap securely. The bagels can be refrigerated for 1–2 days.

For smoked salmon & asparagus bagels, replace the cooked beef with 4 oz smoked salmon and replace the watercress used to flavor the mayonnaise with 1 teaspoon finely grated lemon zest. Toast the bagels as above and fill with the salmon, lemon mayonnaise, and asparagus.

bean, coconut, & spinach soup

Serves **4**

Preparation time **5 minutes**

Cooking time about **20 minutes**

1 tablespoon **olive oil**

1 **onion**, chopped

2 large **garlic cloves**, crushed

1 teaspoon **ground coriander**

2 x 13 oz cans **mixed beans**, drained

13 oz can **coconut milk**

⅔ cup **vegetable stock**

5 cups fresh **spinach**

Heat the oil in a large, heavy saucepan and cook the onion and garlic over a moderate heat for 3–4 minutes until softened. Add the coriander and beans and cook for 1 minute, then add the coconut milk and stock. Bring to a boil, then reduce the heat, cover, and simmer for 10 minutes.

Add the spinach to the pan. Stir well and cook for 5 minutes more.

Whiz the soup in a food processor in 2 batches until smooth, then ladle into warmed serving bowls and serve immediately.

For red lentil & bacon soup, heat 1 tablespoon olive oil and cook 1 chopped onion, 4 oz roughly chopped bacon, 2 large carrots (cut into large chunks), and 1 crushed garlic clove for 3–4 minutes. Add 1¼ cups red lentils, ½ teaspoon ground nutmeg, and 3¾ cups chicken stock and bring to a boil. Reduce the heat, cover, and simmer for 40 minutes until the lentils are soft and cooked. Whiz the soup in a food processor in 2 batches until smooth.

sunset wedges & sour cream

Serves **6**
Preparation time **20 minutes**
Cooking time **30–35 minutes**

3 **sweet potatoes**, skins on
2 large **baking potatoes**,
   skins on
3 tablespoons **olive oil**
1 teaspoon **Cajun spice**
2 tablespoons chopped
   parsley

Dip
⅔ cup **Greek** or **whole milk**
   yogurt
4 tablespoons **sour cream**
4 tablespoons chopped **chives**
2 tablespoons freshly grated
   Parmesan cheese

Cut the sweet potatoes in half, then cut each half into 4 wedges and place in a large mixing bowl. Cut the baking potatoes in half, then cut each half into 6 thick wedges and place in the bowl. Drizzle over the olive oil, then toss well to coat all the potato wedges.

Transfer the potatoes to a large baking sheet or oven tray in a single layer. Sprinkle over the Cajun spice. Roast in a preheated oven, 400°F, for 30–35 minutes until golden and cooked through. Turn onto a serving platter and sprinkle with the parsley.

Mix the yogurt, sour cream, chives, and Parmesan in a small mixing bowl. Serve the dip with the warm potato wedges.

For creamy cucumber & garlic dip to serve as an alternative accompaniment, replace the chives and Parmesan with ¼ grated cucumber and 1 crushed garlic clove. Stir in 2 tablespoons freshly chopped mint and mix well. Serve the dip with the warm potato wedges.

tomato-garlic bread with ham

Serves **2**

Preparation time **10 minutes**

1 **garlic clove**, halved

4 slices **soft white bread**

2 **tomatoes**, 1 halved and
    1 thinly sliced

5 oz finely sliced **ham**

3 oz **Manchego cheese**,
    sliced

Rub the cut faces of the garlic all over the bread, concentrating particularly on the crusts. Repeat with the tomato halves.

Sandwich the bread with the ham, cheese, and sliced tomato. Halve and wrap securely. The sandwiches can be kept in the refrigerator for 1 day.

For tomato-garlic bread with salami & mozzarella, flavor the bread with the garlic and tomato as above and fill with 5 oz finely sliced salami and 3 oz mozzarella. Add 1 sliced tomato. Warm on a baking sheet in a preheated oven, 400°F, for 10 minutes before serving warm, cut into triangles.

pan-fried chicken wraps

Serves **4**
Preparation time **15 minutes**
Cooking time **5 minutes**

2 tablespoons **olive oil**
3 boneless, skinless **chicken breasts**, about 5 oz each, thinly sliced into strips
3 tablespoons **honey**
1 teaspoon **wholegrain mustard**
4 **soft flour tortillas**

Coleslaw

¼ small **white cabbage**, finely shredded
1 large **carrot**, grated
3 tablespoons **olive oil**
2 tablespoons **red wine vinegar**
1 teaspoon **Dijon mustard**
2 tablespoons chopped **parsley**

Make the coleslaw. Put the white cabbage in a large mixing bowl with the carrot and toss together well. In a small bowl beat together the oil, vinegar, and mustard. Pour over the cabbage and carrot and toss well to coat. Add the parsley and toss again. Set aside.

Heat the oil in a large nonstick skillet and cook the chicken strips over a high heat for 4–5 minutes until golden and cooked through. Remove from the heat and add the honey and mustard. Toss well to coat.

Warm the tortillas in a microwave for 10 seconds on high (or in a warm oven), then spread each with the coleslaw and top with the chicken pieces. Wrap each tightly, then cut in half to serve.

For maple-glazed ham wraps, omit the chicken and cut 3 x 6 oz ham steaks into strips. Heat the oil and cook the ham over a high heat for 3–4 minutes until golden and cooked through. Remove from the heat and toss with 3 tablespoons maple syrup (instead of the honey) and the mustard. Assemble the wraps as above.

asparagus in blankets

Serves **4**

Preparation time **10 minutes**

Cooking time **15 minutes**

2 bunches thick **asparagus
spears**, trimmed to about
6 inches long

1 tablespoon **olive oil**

2 tablespoons **butter**,
softened

16 slices **prosciutto** or
serrano ham

4 tablespoons freshly grated
Parmesan cheese

Bring a large pan of water to a boil. Cook the
asparagus for 5 minutes in the boiling water, then
remove with a slotted spoon and place in a bowl.
Toss with the olive oil.

Grease a gratin dish with the butter. Wrap each of
the asparagus spears in a piece of ham and place
them in the greased dish side by side. Sprinkle with
the Parmesan and bake in a preheated oven, 400°F,
for 10 minutes until the cheese is golden and melted.

Serve the asparagus in blankets with chunks of warm
fresh bread and homemade tomato ketchup (see
pages 26–27).

For cheesy pizza-style asparagus, replace the
prosciutto or serrano ham with thin slices of honey-
roast ham and place the wrapped asparagus in the
gratin dish. Sprinkle with 1/3 cup black olives, chopped,
and 1 cup grated mozzarella instead of the Parmesan,
and bake as above. Serve the pizza-style asparagus
with garlic bread.

beanfeast

Serves **4**

Preparation time **10 minutes**

Cooking time **about 15 minutes**

7 oz **tomatoes**

1 tablespoon **vegetable oil**

½ small **onion**, chopped into
small pieces

1 **celery stick**, chopped into
small pieces

2 x 10 oz cans **navy** or
cannellini beans, drained
and rinsed

2 teaspoons **wholegrain
mustard**

2 tablespoons **molasses**

3 tablespoons **tomato ketchup**

1 tablespoon **Worcestershire
sauce**

4 slices **toast** or 4 **baked
potatoes**, to serve

Put the tomatoes into a heatproof bowl and just
cover with freshly boiled water. Allow to stand for
1–2 minutes until the skins start to split. Carefully
pour off the hot water and peel away the skins.
Roughly chop the tomatoes on a cutting board.

Heat the oil in a medium, heavy saucepan for 1 minute.
Add the onion and celery and fry gently for 5 minutes,
stirring until just beginning to brown.

Tip in the beans, tomatoes, mustard, molasses, ketchup,
and Worcestershire sauce and stir the ingredients
together. Heat until the liquid starts to bubble around the
edges. Reduce the heat to its lowest setting and cover
the pan with a lid. Cook gently for about 10 minutes
until the tomatoes have softened to make a sauce.

Serve with toast or on baked potatoes.

For lentil & panir feast, replace the cans of beans
with a 13 oz can puy lentils, drained and rinsed,
and add to the pan with the tomatoes. Cook for
10 minutes, adding 8 oz cubed panir cheese for
the final 2–3 minutes.

chinese-style turkey wraps

Serves **2**
Preparation time **10 minutes**
Cooking time **1–2 minutes**

½ teaspoon **vegetable oil**
4 oz **turkey breast**, thinly
   sliced
1 tablespoon **honey**
2 tablespoons **soy sauce**
1 tablespoon **sesame oil**
2 **soft flour tortillas**
½ cup **bean sprouts**
¼ **red bell pepper**, cored,
   seeded, and thinly sliced
¼ **onion**, thinly sliced
½ cup **snow peas**, sliced
2 **baby corn**, thinly sliced

Heat the oil in a skillet over a moderate heat and add the turkey to the pan. Stir for 1–2 minutes until cooked through. Reduce the heat and stir in the honey, soy sauce, and sesame oil, making sure that the turkey is well coated. Set aside to cool.

Assemble a wrap by placing half the turkey mixture down the center of a tortilla. Add half the bean sprouts and pepper, onion, snow peas, and baby corn. Repeat with the other tortilla. (Alternatively, retain the remaining tortilla and mixture for use another day; the mixture will keep for up to 24 hours in the refrigerator.)

Roll up the tortilla securely and wrap in nonstick parchment paper (plastic wrap can make the wrap rather soggy).

For Chinese-style pork & bok choy wraps, replace the turkey with 4 oz tenderloin pork strips tossed with ½ teaspoon Chinese 5-spice powder and cook as above for 3–4 minutes. Add 1 small head bok choy, shredded with the honey, soy sauce, and sesame oil and cook for an additional 2 minutes. Assemble as above with 1 cup bean sprouts, omitting the snow peas, onion, and corn.

warm seedy rolls

Makes **12**

Preparation time **1 hour 40 minutes**, including resting time

Cooking time **15–20 minutes**

¼ oz active **dried yeast**

1¼ cups **warm water** (not hot)

4 cups **bread flour**, plus extra for dusting

1 teaspoon **salt**, plus a pinch

2 tablespoons **butter**, cut into cubes, plus extra for greasing

4 tablespoons **sunflower seeds**

2 tablespoons **poppy seeds**

2 tablespoons **pumpkin seeds**

1 **egg yolk**

1 tablespoon **water**

Sprinkle the yeast over the measured warm water, stir well and set aside for 10 minutes until it goes frothy. Sift the flour and salt into a large bowl and add the butter. Blend the butter into the flour until the mixture resembles fine bread crumbs. Add all the seeds and stir. Make a well in the center and add the yeast mixture. Stir well with a wooden spoon, then use your hands to mix to a firm dough.

Knead for 5 minutes until the dough feels firm, elastic, and no longer sticky. Return to the bowl, cover with plastic wrap, and set aside in a warm place for 30 minutes until the dough has doubled in size.

Turn out the dough and knead again to knock out the air, then divide into 12 pieces. Knead each piece briefly, then form into a roll shape, or roll each piece into a long sausage shape and form into a loose knot. Place the rolls on a lightly greased baking sheet, cover with a clean dish towel and set aside in a warm place for 30 minutes until almost doubled in size.

Mix the egg yolk in a small bowl with a pinch of salt and the measured water and brush over the rolls to glaze. Bake in a preheated oven, 400°F, for 15–20 minutes until golden and sounding hollow when tapped lightly on the base. Remove from the oven and allow to cool a little. Serve warm with soup.

For cheesy onion rolls, replace the seeds with 5 scallions, very finely chopped and lightly cooked for just 1 minute in 1 tablespoon olive oil. Once glazed, sprinkle with 3 tablespoons freshly grated Parmesan cheese.

roasted vegetable couscous

Serves **6**
Preparation time **15 minutes**,
  plus soaking
Cooking time **30–35 minutes**

1 cup **couscous**
1 **chicken bouillon cube**
1¾ cups **hot water**
2 **zucchini**, cut into chunks
1 **red bell pepper**, cored,
  seeded, and cut into chunks
1 **yellow bell pepper**, cored,
  seeded, and cut into chunks
12 oz **butternut squash**,
  peeled, seeded, and cut
  into chunks
1 **red onion**, chopped
5 tablespoons **olive oil**
3 tablespoons chopped
  parsley or **basil**
5 tablespoons **pine nuts**,
  toasted

Place the couscous in a bowl, crumble in the bouillon cube and stir well. Add the measured water, stir, then cover and set aside, while preparing and cooking the vegetables, to soak and swell.

Put all the prepared vegetables into a large roasting pan and drizzle over 3 tablespoons of the oil and toss to coat lightly. Roast in a preheated oven, 400°F, for 30–35 minutes until the vegetables are soft and lightly charred.

Lightly fork the soaked couscous to fluff it up, then drizzle over the remaining oil and toss well. Add the warm vegetables, parsley or basil, and pine nuts and toss well before serving.

For roasted vegetable quinoa with toasted cashews, replace the couscous with quinoa. Wash 1 cup quinoa in a sieve, then drain. Place in a large, heavy nonstick skillet and lightly toast over a moderate heat for 2–3 minutes until the grain turns a shade darker. Add 1¾ cups water and 1 chicken bouillon cube and cook over a moderate heat for 8–10 minutes until the grain is tender and cooked. Drain and set aside. Add the roasted vegetables and parsley as above and replace the pine nuts with ⅔ cup roughly chopped toasted cashews.

peking wraps

Serves **2**
Preparation time **10 minutes**
Cooking time **about**
  10 minutes

1 **duck breast**, weighing about
  6 oz, with skin, cut across
  into very thin slices
½ teaspoon **Chinese 5-spice**
  powder
1 tablespoon **vegetable oil**
2 large **soft flour tortillas**
2 tablespoons **hoisin sauce**
2 **iceberg lettuce leaves**,
  thinly shredded
2 inch piece **cucumber**, sliced
  into matchstick-size pieces
2 **scallions**, thinly sliced
  diagonally

Put the slices of duck on a plate and sprinkle with
the 5-spice powder. Turn the slices in the spice until
coated all over. Heat the oil in a small skillet for
1 minute. Add the duck and fry gently for 5 minutes,
turning the pieces with a spatula. Using the spatula,
transfer the duck to a plate and allow to cool while
you prepare the filling.

Heat the tortillas one at a time in the microwave on full
power for 8 seconds. Alternatively, warm them under a
hot broiler or in a skillet for approximately 10 seconds.

Spread the hoisin sauce over one side of each tortilla.
Scatter a line of lettuce, then the cucumber, scallions,
and duck down the center of each tortilla, keeping the
ingredients away from the ends.

Fold 2 sides of each tortilla over the ends of the filling,
then roll them up tightly from an unfolded side so that
the filling is completely enclosed. Cut the wraps in half,
wrap in nonstick parchment paper, and chill in the
refrigerator until ready to go.

For crispy lamb & lettuce Peking wraps, toss 6 oz
lamb loin strips in the 5-spice powder and cook as
above. Use shredded lettuce, scallion, and cucumber
as before, as well as strips of finely sliced carrot.

tuna melts

Serves **2**
Preparation time **10 minutes**
Cooking time **11–13 minutes**

7 oz can **tuna**, in oil or brine,
   drained
½ cup frozen **corn kernels**
3 tablespoons **mayonnaise**
2 **panini**, cut in half horizontally
3 oz **Gruyère** or **Emmental**
   cheese, thinly sliced

Flake the tuna into a bowl. Put the corn in a small saucepan and pour boiling water over to just cover it. Cook for 3 minutes and drain through a sieve. Rinse the corn under cold water and add it to the tuna. Stir in the mayonnaise until well mixed.

Spread the tuna mixture over the two bread bases. Arrange the cheese on top of the tuna. Press the bread tops down firmly on the filling.

Heat a heavy skillet or ridged griddle pan for 2 minutes. Add the breads and cook on a gentle heat for 3–4 minutes on each side, turning them carefully with a spatula or tongs. Wrap the tuna melts in nonstick parchment paper and chill in the refridgerator until ready to serve.

For warm haloumi & vegetable melts, heat 1 tablespoon olive oil in a skillet and cook 1 small, thinly sliced zucchini and 1 thinly sliced red bell pepper for 3–4 minutes until softened. Fill the paninis with the vegetables and top with 4 oz thinly sliced haloumi cheese. Cook as above, then transfer to serving plates and serve.

baked sweet potatoes & shrimp

Serves **4**

Preparation time **10 minutes**

Cooking time **25–30 minutes**

1 tablespoon **olive oil**

4 large **sweet potatoes**, skin on, scrubbed, patted dry

8 oz medium **shrimp**, defrosted if frozen

1 ripe **avocado**, cut into small chunks

2 tablespoons **mayonnaise**

2 tablespoons **milk** or **water**

3 tablespoons **sour cream**

1 tablespoon **tomato paste**

To serve

ground paprika

1 small pot **sprouting alfalfa** (or other sprouting seeds)

Drizzle a little of the oil over each sweet potato, then rub it all over the skin. Put the potatoes on a baking sheet. Bake in a preheated oven, 400°F, for 25–30 minutes until tender and cooked through.

Meanwhile, place the shrimp and avocado in a bowl and toss together. Mix the mayonnaise with the milk or water until smooth, then add the sour cream and tomato paste and mix until well blended. Add the shrimp and avocado and toss well to coat lightly.

Remove the sweet potatoes from the oven. Split the hot potatoes and fill them with the shrimp mixture. Serve garnished with a pinch of paprika and some freshly cut sprouting seeds.

For baked sweet potatoes & creamy mushrooms,

bake the sweet potatoes as above. Heat 1 tablespoon olive oil in a heavy skillet and cook 8 oz quartered chestnut mushrooms over a high heat for 3–4 minutes until golden and softened. Remove from the heat, add ¾ cup sour cream and 1 teaspoon Dijon mustard and stir well for a few seconds until piping hot. Spoon into the sweet potatoes as above.

spicy chorizo wrap

Serves **2**

Preparation time **15 minutes**

Cooking time **5–7 minutes**

4 eggs

½ teaspoon **mild chili powder**

2 oz sliced **chorizo sausage**,
  cut into thin shreds

2 tablespoons **olive oil**

1 container **cress**

2 large **soft flour tortillas**

2 tablespoons **red pesto**

Break the eggs into a bowl and add the chili powder.
Beat well until the eggs are completely broken up.
Stir in the chorizo. Heat the oil in a small skillet for
1 minute. Tip the egg mixture into the pan. When the
eggs start to set around the edges, use a fork to push
the cooked parts into the center of the pan so the
uncooked egg flows into the space. Keep doing this
until the eggs are no longer runny, then let the omelet
cook until just set (3–5 minutes). Slide the omelet onto
a plate and allow to cool.

Cut the cress from the container and put it in a sieve.
Rinse under cold water and let drain.

Prepare the tortillas by heating in the microwave on full
power for 10 seconds. Alternatively, warm them under
a hot broiler or heat in the skillet for approximately
10 seconds (wipe out the pan with paper towels first,
taking care as it might still be hot).

Spread one side of each of the tortillas with the pesto.
Cut the omelet in half and place one half on top of
each tortilla, then sprinkle with the cress. Roll up tightly
so the filling is completely enclosed. Cut the wraps in
half, wrap in nonstick parchment paper and chill in the
refrigerator until ready to serve.

For pesto chicken wraps, replace the chorizo with
3 oz cooked and torn chicken pieces and ⅓ cup black
olives, sliced. Spread the tortilla with 1 tablespoon
green pesto and top with the omelet. Omit the cress,
roll up, and serve warm.

delicious dinners

green cheese pasta

Serves **4**
Preparation time **10 minutes**
Cooking time **10 minutes**

8 oz **pasta shapes**
6 cups fresh **spinach**
1 teaspoon **ground nutmeg**
¼ cup **butter**
½ cup **all-purpose flour**
2½ cups **milk**
1 cup grated **cheddar cheese**

Cook the pasta shapes for 8–10 minutes or according to package instructions until just tender. Drain and set aside.

Meanwhile, place the spinach in a pan of boiling water and cook, stirring continuously, over a moderate heat for 2 minutes until wilted. Remove from the heat and drain well, then return to the pan and toss with the nutmeg. Set aside.

Melt the butter in a medium, heavy saucepan. Remove from the heat, add the flour, and stir to form a thick paste. Return to the heat and cook gently for a few seconds, stirring continuously. Remove from the heat and gradually add the milk, stirring well after each addition. Return to the heat and bring to a boil, stirring continuously until the sauce has boiled and thickened.

Remove from the heat and add the spinach and cheese. Stir, then transfer to a food processor and whiz until smooth. Return to the pan and add the pasta. Stir well to coat, then divide between 4 warmed serving bowls.

For zucchini & garlic pasta, replace the spinach with 3 large zucchini, trimmed and grated. Heat 1 tablespoon olive oil in a nonstick skillet and cook the zucchini and 1 crushed garlic clove over a moderate heat for 4–5 minutes until soft and tender. Add 3 tablespoons of chopped chives, then add to the sauce in place of the spinach and whiz until smooth before tossing with the pasta.

chicken rice salad

Serves **4**
Preparation time **10 minutes**,
   plus cooling
Cooking time **about**
   15 minutes

4 **chicken thighs**, skinned
   and boned
¾ cup **long-grain rice**
2 teaspoons **lemon juice**
2 tablespoons **peanut butter**
   (optional)
2 tablespoons **olive oil**
2 **pineapple rings**, chopped
1 **red bell pepper**, cored,
   seeded, and chopped
½ cup **sugar snap peas**,
   sliced
4 tablespoons **peanuts**
   (optional)

Place the chicken thighs in a steamer set over boiling water for 10–12 minutes until cooked through. Alternatively, simmer them in shallow water in a skillet for 10 minutes. Remove from the steamer or pan and set aside to cool.

Meanwhile, cook the rice according to the package instructions. Drain and rinse under cold water to cool the rice completely, then tip it into a large bowl.

Make the dressing: mix together the lemon juice and peanut butter, if using, until well combined, then beat in the oil.

Dice the chicken thighs into bite-size pieces and stir into the rice. Add the pineapple, bell pepper, sugar snap peas, and peanuts, if using. Pour the dressing over the chicken rice salad and serve.

For shrimp rice salad, make up the peanut dressing as above. Replace the chicken with 5 oz shrimp tossed with 2 tablespoons toasted sesame seeds. Cut ¼ cucumber into thin sticks and toss with the rice, peanut sauce, shrimp, and seeds.

salmon pasta bake

Serves **6**

Preparation time **20 minutes**

Cooking time **30 minutes**

8 oz **pasta shapes**

2 tablespoons **butter**

¼ cup **all-purpose flour**

1¼ cups **milk**

¾ cup **sour cream**

1 cup freshly grated
Parmesan cheese

3 tablespoons chopped **herbs**
(such as chives or dill weed)

2 x 7 oz cans **red salmon**,
drained and flaked

⅔ cup frozen **peas**

Cook the pasta for 8–10 minutes or according to package instructions until tender. Drain and set aside.

Heat the butter in a nonstick pan until melted. Remove from the heat, add the flour, and stir well to form a thick paste. Return the pan to the heat and cook, stirring continuously, for 1 minute. Remove from the heat and gradually add the milk, a little at a time, stirring well until all the milk is used.

Return the pan to the heat and bring to a boil, stirring continuously until boiled and thickened. Add the sour cream and half the Parmesan and stir well. Add the drained pasta, herbs, flaked salmon, and peas and toss gently to mix, taking care not to break up the fish. Transfer to 6 individual gratin dishes and sprinkle over the remaining Parmesan.

Bake in a preheated oven, 350°F, for 20 minutes until golden and bubbling. Serve with warm bread and a simple salad.

For tuna pasta bake with corn, replace the salmon with 2 x 7 oz cans of tuna in brine, drained and flaked, and replace the peas with ⅔ cup corn kernels. Add 1 tablespoon wholegrain mustard and mix well. Cut a garlic baguette into slices and place on top of the pasta. Sprinkle with the remaining Parmesan and bake as above until the bread is crisp and golden and the sauce is bubbling.

spaghetti bolognaise

Serves **6**
Preparation time **30 minutes**
Cooking time **35 minutes**

2 tablespoons **olive oil**
1 **onion**, finely chopped
2 **carrots**, grated
1 **zucchini**, grated
1 lb **lean ground beef**
2 tablespoons **all-purpose flour**
2 tablespoons **tomato paste**
2½ cups **rich beef stock**
7 oz can **chopped tomatoes**
8 oz **spaghetti** or **linguine**
freshly grated **Parmesan cheese**, to serve

Heat 1 tablespoon of the oil in a large, heavy saucepan and cook the onion, carrots, and zucchini over a moderate heat for 5–6 minutes, stirring occasionally until soft. Remove the vegetables from the pan and set aside.

Add the beef to the pan and cook over a high heat for 4–5 minutes, stirring frequently until browned all over. Return the vegetables to the pan, add the flour, and stir well to coat lightly. Add the tomato paste to the beef stock and stir well, then add the stock to the meat along with the chopped tomatoes. Bring to a boil, then reduce the heat, cover with a lid, and simmer for 20 minutes.

Meanwhile, cook the pasta for 8–10 minutes or according to package instructions until tender. Drain and toss with the remaining oil. Arrange the pasta in warmed serving bowls and pile the bolognaise sauce on top. Sprinkle with the Parmesan.

For bolognaise pasta bake, cook 8 oz macaroni until just tender. Drain and toss with 1 tablespoon olive oil. Make up the bolognaise sauce as above and mix with the macaroni. Transfer to a large gratin dish. Mix ¾ cup sour cream with 3 tablespoons freshly grated Parmesan cheese and 2 tablespoons chopped parsley, and spoon over the top of the macaroni. Bake in a preheated oven, 400°F, for 20–25 minutes until the topping is golden and bubbling.

potato & cheese röstis

Makes **4**
Preparation time **10 minutes**
Cooking time **25 minutes**

1 lb **red** or **waxy potatoes**,
  unpeeled
½ cup grated **mild cheddar
  cheese**
1 **red onion**, finely chopped
3 tablespoons **vegetable oil**
Tomato Ketchup (see pages
  26–27), to serve

Put the potatoes in a large pan of water and bring to
a boil. Boil for about 20 minutes until the potatoes are
just cooked but firm. Drain and cool.

Peel the potatoes and grate them into a bowl. Stir in
the grated cheddar and onion. With wet hands, shape
into 4 rounds, then press down with 2 fingers to form
into röstis. Neaten up the edges.

Brush lightly with oil on both sides and broil on a
foil-lined broiler rack at a medium heat for 2–3 minutes
on each side until golden brown.

Serve the röstis warm with the ketchup. (Any that are
not needed straight away may be stored in an airtight
container in the refrigerator for up to 3 days.)

For potato, bacon, & tomato röstis, make the potato
mixture as above, omitting the onion. Add 1 finely
chopped large tomato and 2 slices finely chopped
cooked bacon to the mixture along with 2 tablespoons
tomato ketchup. Shape into 4 patties and cook as
above. Use to fill warm toasted whole-wheat pita
breads with watercress and extra ketchup.

sweet potato-topped fish pie

Serves **4**
Preparation time **45 minutes**
Cooking time **45 minutes**

12 oz **cod fillet**
1¼ cups **water**
8 oz **shrimp**, thawed if frozen,
   drained
1 large **carrot**, roughly
   chopped
8 oz **broccoli**, cut into small
   florets
2 tablespoons **butter**
¼ cup **all-purpose flour**
1¼ cups **milk**
½ cup grated **cheddar cheese**

Potato topping
1¼ lb **sweet potatoes**, peeled
   and chopped
¼ cup **butter**
3 tablespoons chopped
   parsley
¼ cup finely grated **cheddar
   cheese**

Place the cod fillet in a medium, heavy skillet and pour over the measured water. Bring to a boil, reduce the heat, cover, and simmer for 3 minutes until the fish is opaque and cooked through. Drain and reserve the fish stock. Flake the fish into chunks and gently toss with the shrimp.

Cook the carrot and broccoli in boiling water for 5 minutes, drain, and set aside. Melt the butter in a pan, remove from the heat, and add the flour. Stir over a gentle heat for 30 seconds. Remove from the heat and gradually add the milk a little at a time, stirring well after each addition, then add the reserved fish stock and stir well.

Return the pan to the heat and bring to a boil, stirring continuously until thickened. Remove from the heat and add the cheddar. Pour over the fish, add the vegetables, and very gently fold together. Transfer to a large gratin dish and set aside.

Meanwhile, cook the sweet potatoes for 8–10 minutes until tender. Drain, add the butter, and mash well. Stir in the parsley, spoon over the top of the fish and sauce, and sprinkle with the cheddar. Bake in a preheated oven, 400°F, for 30 minutes until a golden crust forms.

For cheesy tuna & shrimp pie, replace the cod with 2 x 7 oz cans tuna in brine, drained and flaked. Cook 1½ lb white potatoes and mash with the butter, an extra ½ cup cheddar and 6 tablespoons milk. Fold in the parsley, spoon over the pie, sprinkle with the remaining cheese, and bake as above.

asian noodles with shrimp

Serves **2**
Preparation time **20 minutes**
Cooking time **10 minutes**

3 tablespoons **plum sauce**
2 tablespoons **seasoned rice vinegar**
2 tablespoons **soy sauce**
4 oz fine or medium **egg noodles**
1 tablespoon **vegetable oil**
2 **scallions**, sliced diagonally into chunky pieces
½ mild **red chili**, cored, seeded, and finely chopped
1 cup thinly sliced **bok choy** or **cabbage**
4 oz **baby corn**, cut in half diagonally
7 oz peeled **shrimp**, thawed if frozen, drained

Mix the plum sauce with the rice vinegar and soy sauce in a small bowl and set aside.

Pour plenty of freshly boiled water into a medium saucepan and bring back to a boil. Add the noodles and cook for 3 minutes. Drain through a colander.

Heat the oil in a large skillet or wok for 1 minute. Add the scallions and chili and fry for 1 minute, stirring with a wooden spoon. Add the bok choy or cabbage and the corn and fry for 2–3 minutes more until the vegetables are softened.

Tip the noodles, shrimp, and sauce into the pan and cook, stirring gently, over a low heat until the ingredients are mixed together and hot. Serve immediately.

For Asian noodles with beef & coconut, replace the red chili and bok choy with ¾ cup blanched broccoli florets. Add to the wok with the scallions and cook for 1 minute. Add 6 oz sirloin steak, cut into thin strips and cook in the pan for an additional 2–3 minutes until golden. Add 1¾ cups coconut milk with 2 tablespoons soy sauce to replace the plum sauce and toss with the noodles. Heat for 1 minute until hot.

salmon rösti cakes

Serves **6**
Preparation time **30 minutes**
Cooking time **25–30 minutes**

1 lb **white potatoes**, peeled
    but left whole
2 tablespoons **butter**
8 oz **salmon fillets**
2 tablespoons **sunflower oil**
¾ cup **sour cream**
3 **scallions**, finely sliced
2 tablespoons chopped **chives**
lemon wedges, to serve

Bring a large pan of lightly salted water to a boil. Cook the potatoes for 10 minutes until beginning to soften. Drain and set aside to cool.

Heat the butter in a small skillet and add the salmon. Cover with a tight-fitting lid and reduce the heat to very low. Cook for 8–10 minutes until the salmon is just cooked. Remove from the heat and set aside until the salmon is cool enough to handle. Flake the salmon and place in a bowl with the pan juices.

Grate the cooled potatoes, add to the bowl with the salmon and toss together to mix. Divide the mixture into 6 and form into flattened patty shapes. Heat the oil in a large nonstick skillet and cook the rösti over a moderate heat for 2–3 minutes on each side until golden and cooked through, turning with a spatula.

Meanwhile, place the sour cream in a bowl with the scallions and chives and mix well. Drain the rösti on paper towels, then spoon over the sour cream and serve with lemon wedges.

For rösti with bacon & eggs, follow the recipe above, omitting the salmon and adding 1 tablespoon chopped parsley before shaping. Serve the crisp rösti each with 2 lightly fried bacon slices and a poached egg on top, and homemade ketchup (see pages 26–27).

crumb-topped macaroni & cheese

Serves **4**
Preparation time **15 minutes**
Cooking time **about**
  25 minutes

7 oz **macaroni**
⅔ cup fresh or frozen **peas**
5 tablespoons **butter**
6 tablespoons **all-purpose flour**
2 cups **milk**
1 teaspoon **Dijon mustard**
1½ cups coarsely grated **cheddar cheese**
4 oz **ham**, chopped into small pieces
1¼ cups **bread crumbs**

Cook the macaroni for about 10 minutes or according to package instructions until just tender. Add the peas to the pan and cook for 2 minutes more. Drain and put on one side.

Melt 3 tablespoons of the butter in the rinsed and dried saucepan. Add the flour and stir it in with a wooden spoon. Cook over a gentle heat, stirring, for 1 minute. Remove the pan from the heat and gradually pour in the milk, beating well. Return the pan to the heat and cook over a gentle heat, stirring continuously until the sauce is thickened and smooth.

Add the mustard, cheddar, and ham and stir until the cheese has melted. Tip in the macaroni and peas and stir until coated in the sauce, then pour into a shallow heatproof dish.

Melt the remaining butter in a small saucepan and stir in the bread crumbs until they are coated. Sprinkle the bread crumbs over the macaroni and cook under a moderate broiler for about 5 minutes or until golden, watching closely as the bread crumbs will brown quickly. Use an oven mitt to remove the dish from under the broiler, and serve.

For crumb-topped eggplant & macaroni and cheese, omit the peas and ham and replace with half a roughly chopped eggplant cooked in 2 tablespoons olive oil until soft, and 3 roughly chopped tomatoes. Top with the crumbs and bake as above.

korma-style curried shrimp

Serves **4**
Preparation time **5 minutes**
Cooking time **about**
  25 minutes

1 tablespoon **vegetable oil**
1 **onion**, roughly chopped
½ inch piece **ginger root**,
  peeled and finely grated
1 teaspoon **ground coriander**
½ teaspoon **ground cumin**
½ teaspoon **curry powder**
13 oz can **chopped tomatoes**
1 tablespoon **brown sugar**
1¾ cups **coconut milk**
8 oz **shrimp**, thawed if frozen
⅔ cup frozen **peas**
3 tablespoons chopped
  cilantro
rice or **naan**, to serve

Heat the oil in a large nonstick skillet and cook the onion and ginger over a gentle heat for 3–4 minutes, stirring regularly until soft, but not golden. Add the spices and cook for 1 minute more. Add the chopped tomatoes and sugar and increase the heat slightly, continuing to cook for an additional 5 minutes, stirring occasionally, until the tomatoes have reduced slightly and thickened.

Pour in the coconut milk and bring to a boil. Reduce the heat and simmer, uncovered, for 10 minutes until the sauce has reduced and thickened. Drain the shrimp well, then add to the sauce with the peas and cilantro and cook for 2–3 minutes more until piping hot.

Serve the mild curry in warmed serving bowls, with either rice or naan breads to mop up the juices.

For mild chicken & squash curry, omit the ginger and replace the shrimp with 8 oz roughly chopped chicken breast and the peas with 8 oz butternut squash, peeled and cubed. Cook both the chicken and the squash with the onion as above, then add the spices and continue to follow the remaining recipe as above.

lamb hotpot with dumplings

Serves **4**
Preparation time **30 minutes**
Cooking time **about 1 hour**

1 tablespoon **vegetable oil**
1 small **onion**, chopped
12 oz boneless **lamb**, cubed
1 **leek**, chopped
½ cup ready-to-eat **dried apricots**, chopped
12 oz **new potatoes**, halved
1 tablespoon **thyme leaves**
2 tablespoons **all-purpose flour**
2½ cups **rich lamb stock**

Dumplings
1 cup **all-purpose flour**
½ teaspoon **salt**
1 teaspoon **thyme leaves**
½ cup **vegetable suet**
about 4 tablespoons cold **water**

Heat the oil in a large, heavy saucepan and cook the onion and lamb over a moderate heat for 4–5 minutes until golden and soft. Add the leek, apricots, and new potatoes and cook for 2 minutes, then add the thyme and flour and stir well to coat lightly. Pour in the stock, then bring to a boil and cover and simmer gently for 35 minutes, stirring occasionally.

Meanwhile, make the dumplings. Place the flour and salt in a bowl with the thyme leaves and suet and mix well. Mix in enough water to make an elastic dough. Divide into 12 and shape into small walnut-size balls using lightly floured hands. Stir the hotpot and top up with a little water if necessary, then drop the dumplings into the stock and cover and simmer for 15 minutes until the dumplings have almost doubled in size.

Serve the hotpot ladled into warm serving bowls with the dumplings.

For vegetable hotpot with cheesy dumplings,

omit the lamb and replace with 2 chopped carrots, 1 roughly chopped red bell pepper and 1 chopped zucchini. Also replace the lamb stock with vegetable stock, and cook as above. Add 3 tablespoons raisins with the apricots. Add ¼ cup finely grated cheddar cheese to the all-purpose flour when making the dumplings and cook as above.

all-in-one chicken pie

Serves **4**
Preparation time **20 minutes**
Cooking time **45–50 minutes**

1 cup **broccoli florets**
1 tablespoon **olive oil**
12 oz boneless, skinless
   chicken breasts, cubed
6 **bacon** slices, chopped
2 small **carrots**, chopped
2 tablespoons **butter**
¼ cup **all-purpose flour**
1¼ cups **milk**
1 tablespoon **white wine
   vinegar**
1 teaspoon **Dijon mustard**
¾ cup **sour cream**
2 tablespoons chopped
   tarragon or **parsley**
1 lb package **short pastry**
beaten **egg**, for glazing

Cook the broccoli for 5 minutes until tender. Drain and refresh with cold water, then set aside. Heat the oil in a nonstick skillet and cook the chicken and bacon over a moderate heat for 7–8 minutes. Add the carrots and cook for an additional 3–4 minutes until golden all over. Remove from the heat.

Heat the butter in a medium saucepan and add the flour. Cook over a gentle heat for a few seconds, then remove from the heat and gradually add the milk until well mixed. Add the vinegar and mustard and mix well. Return to the heat and stir continuously until boiled and thickened. Add the sour cream and herbs. Add the chicken and vegetables and stir well to coat, then transfer to a round pie dish.

Roll out the pastry on a floured surface to just larger than the dish. Moisten the rim of the dish lightly with a little water, then place the pastry over the top, trim the edges, and decorate with any remaining pastry trimmings if desired. Glaze lightly with the beaten egg. Bake in a preheated oven, 350°F, for 25–30 minutes until crisp and golden.

For creamy chunky ham pie, replace the chicken and bacon with a 1 lb ham joint. Half fill a large pan with water, then add 3 peppercorns and a bay leaf. Lower the ham into the pan, then bring to a boil and cook for 1½ hours. Drain and set aside to cool. Cook the carrots with the broccoli, then cut the ham into chunks and add the vegetables and ham to the sauce. Continue as above.

baked cabbage with nuts & cheese

Serves **4**
Preparation time **15 minutes**
Cooking time **30 minutes**

3 cups shredded **white cabbage**
1 cup shredded **green** or **savoy cabbage**
1 teaspoon **ground nutmeg**
½ cup roasted unsalted **peanuts**, toasted
2 tablespoons **butter**
¼ cup **all-purpose flour**
1¾ cups **milk**
1 cup grated sharp **cheddar cheese**
1 teaspoon **Dijon mustard**
2 tablespoons chopped **parsley**
½ cup **whole-wheat bread crumbs**

Cook the two types of cabbage in boiling water for 5 minutes until just tender. Drain and place in a large mixing bowl and toss with the nutmeg and peanuts.

Heat the butter in a nonstick saucepan until melted. Remove from the heat, add the flour, and mix to a paste. Return to the heat and cook for a few seconds. Remove from the heat and add the milk a little at a time, stirring well between each addition. Return to the heat and bring to a boil, stirring continuously until boiled and thickened.

Remove the pan from the heat and add three-quarters of the grated cheddar and the mustard. Mix well, then pour over the cabbage and mix it in.

Transfer the mixture to a gratin dish, or 4 individual gratin dishes. Toss the remaining cheese with the parsley and bread crumbs, then sprinkle over the top and bake in a preheated oven, 400°F, for 20 minutes until golden and bubbling.

For root vegetable bake with nuts & cheese,
replace the cabbage with 1½ cups sliced butternut squash and 1 cup sliced parsnips. Cook in boiling water for 5 minutes and drain. Mix with the nuts and cheese sauce, sprinkle with the cheesy bread crumbs, and bake as above.

supper in a hurry

Serves **4**

Preparation time **25 minutes**

Cooking time **20 minutes**

1 **ciabatta bread loaf**

small handful **chives**

½ cup **garlic butter**, softened

5 tablespoons **olive oil**

4 boneless, skinless **chicken breasts**, cut in half horizontally

4 **tomatoes**, sliced

5 oz **mozzarella cheese**, drained and sliced

1 tablespoon **white wine vinegar**

1 tablespoon **wholegrain mustard**

1 teaspoon **superfine sugar**

Cut the bread at ¾ inch intervals, leaving the slices only just attached at the base.

Snip the chives with scissors and mix half in a bowl with the garlic butter. Roughly spread a dot of butter into each cut of the bread. Lay the loaf on a piece of foil and bring the edges up over the top, scrunching them together. Bake in a preheated oven, 425°F, for 10 minutes.

Meanwhile, heat 1 tablespoon of the oil in a large skillet. Add the chicken and fry gently for 5 minutes until golden on the underside (check by lifting a piece with a spatula). Turn the pieces over and fry for 5 minutes more.

Using an oven mitt, carefully open out the foil on the garlic bread and bake for an additional 10 minutes.

Arrange the tomato and mozzarella slices in a shallow dish.

Make a dressing by beating together the remaining oil with the vinegar, mustard, and sugar in a bowl. Sprinkle the remaining chives over the salad and drizzle with the dressing. Using an oven mitt, remove the garlic bread from the oven and serve with the salad and chicken.

For speedy breaded pork scallops, lightly toss 4 pork scallops in a little flour, dip in 4 beaten eggs and then coat in 4 cups whole-wheat bread crumbs tossed with 2 pinches smoked paprika. Heat 3 tablespoons oil in a nonstick skillet and cook the scallops for 2–3 minutes on each side until golden. Serve with the tomato and mozzarella salad as above.

butternut squash risotto

Serves **4**
Preparation time **15 minutes**
Cooking time **about
  25 minutes**

2 tablespoons **olive oil**
1 **onion**, finely chopped
1 lb **butternut squash**, peeled,
   seeded, and roughly chopped
1¼ cups **arborio rice**
3¾ cups **rich chicken stock**
¾ cup freshly grated
   Parmesan cheese, plus
   extra to serve
4 tablespoons **pine nuts**,
   toasted
5 cups fresh **spinach leaves**

Heat the oil in a large heavy skillet and cook the onion and squash over a low to moderate heat for 10 minutes until softened. Add the rice and cook for 1 minute, then add half the stock. Bring to a boil, then reduce the heat and simmer gently for 5 minutes until almost all the stock has been absorbed, stirring occasionally.

Continue to add the stock ½ cup at a time and cook over a gentle heat until almost all the stock has been absorbed before adding more. Once the rice is tender, remove the pan from the heat, add the Parmesan, pine nuts, and spinach and stir well to combine and wilt the spinach, returning to the heat for 1 minute if necessary.

Serve in warmed serving bowls with extra freshly grated Parmesan.

For chicken & pea risotto, replace the butternut squash with 3 x 5 oz chicken breasts, chopped and cooked with the onion. Cook in the same way as above, adding an additional 1 cup frozen peas and adding the spinach if desired. Serve with extra Parmesan sprinkled over.

on-the-run suppers

tasty teatime pasties

Makes **6**

Preparation time **25 minutes**, plus chilling

Cooking time **25 minutes**

3 cups **all-purpose flour**
½ teaspoon **salt**
¾ cup **butter**, cubed
2–3 tablespoons cold **water**
1 tablespoon **vegetable oil**
½ small **onion**, chopped
6 oz lean **lamb**, finely sliced
1 small **potato** or 2 **baby new potatoes**, peeled and diced
1¼ cups hot **lamb stock**
1 teaspoon **Dijon mustard**, optional
2 tablespoons finely chopped **mint**
beaten **egg**

Sift the flour and salt into a large mixing bowl and add the butter. Blend the butter into the flour until the mixture resembles fine bread crumbs. Add the measured water and mix to form a rough dough. Turn onto a lightly floured work surface and knead until smooth. Place in a food bag and refrigerate for 30 minutes.

Meanwhile, heat the oil in a skillet and cook the onion and lamb over a moderate heat for 5 minutes, stirring occasionally, until beginning to brown. Add the potato, reduce the heat, and cook for an additional 2 minutes, stirring occasionally until beginning to brown.

Mix the lamb stock with the mustard and pour into the pan. Cover with a tight-fitting lid and simmer gently for 15 minutes, stirring occasionally until the potatoes are soft yet still retaining their shape, and the meat is tender. Stir in the mint and set aside to cool.

Roll out the pastry to ¼ inch thick, and using a 6 inch saucer as a template, cut out 6 rounds. Lightly brush the edges of each of the circles with a little water and place 2 tablespoons of the mixture in the center of each. Fold up to enclose the filling and pinch and gently twist the edges to seal. Place on a baking sheet and lightly glaze each one with the beaten egg. Bake in a preheated oven, 400°F, for 20–25 minutes until the pastry is golden and crisp. Wrap loosely in foil to keep warm.

spanish tortilla

Serves **8**
Preparation time **10 minutes**
Cooking time **20–25 minutes**

2 tablespoons **olive oil**
2 **onions**, sliced
1 **garlic clove**, crushed
1 lb cooked **waxy potatoes**,
  sliced
6 **eggs**
3 tablespoons **milk**

Heat 1 tablespoon of the olive oil in a medium skillet, with a metal handle, over a low heat and add the onions and garlic. Cook for 5 minutes until golden, then add the cooked potatoes and heat through.

Meanwhile, in a large bowl, beat together the eggs and milk. Add the potatoes, onion, and garlic to the egg mixture and stir well.

Return the pan to the heat, and heat the remaining oil. Tip the potato and egg mixture into the pan and cook over a low heat for 7–8 minutes, until beginning to set. Preheat the broiler to a medium heat and cook the tortilla in its pan under the broiler for 3–5 minutes until the top is golden and set.

Turn out the tortilla onto a plate and allow to cool. Cut into slices and serve warm or cold. (You can wrap any unused tortilla securely and refrigerate it—eat within 3 days.)

For meaty chorizo Spanish tortilla, layer the potatoes with 3 oz sliced chorizo and 2 tablespoons chopped parsley and cook as above. Serve either warm or cold with cherry tomatoes.

mini quiches

Makes **18**
Preparation time **45 minutes**
Cooking time **20 minutes**

vegetable oil, for greasing
all-purpose flour, for dusting
12 oz ready-rolled **short
    pastry**, thawed if frozen and
    taken out of the refrigerator
    15 minutes before use
2 **eggs**
¾ cup **milk**
4 slices **ham**, diced
2 **scallions**, chopped
5 **cherry tomatoes**, chopped
½ cup grated **cheddar cheese**

Smear some oil around the cups of 2 bun pans.
Sprinkle some flour onto a work surface and unroll the
pastry. Flatten it with the balls of your hands. Stamp
circles out of the pastry with a cutter and place each
circle in a cup of the pan, gently pressing it down with
your fingertips.

Place the eggs and milk in a measuring cup and beat
with a fork.

Put the ham, scallions, and cherry tomatoes in a bowl
and mix together. Put a dessertspoonful of the mixture
into each pastry cup.

Pour some of the egg and milk mixture into each cup.
Sprinkle some cheddar over the top. Bake the quiches
in a preheated oven, 425°F, for 20 minutes or until set
and golden. Serve the quiches hot or cold.

For red pepper, garlic, & Parmesan quiches, replace
the ham, scallions, and cherry tomatoes with the
following—heat 1 tablespoon olive oil in a small pan
and cook 1 roughly chopped red bell pepper and
1 crushed garlic clove for 2–3 minutes until soft.
Place in the pastry shells with ½ cup freshly grated
Parmesan cheese and pour over the egg and milk as
above. Omit the cheddar and bake as above.

no-mess cheesy pepperoni calzones

Serves **8**
Preparation time **30–40
minutes**
Cooking time **25–30 minutes**

10 oz **pizza dough mix**
flour, for dusting
1 tablespoon **olive oil**
1 small **red bell pepper**,
cored, seeded, and roughly
chopped
1 small **yellow bell pepper**,
cored, seeded, and roughly
chopped
6 oz **chorizo sausage**, sliced
1 large **tomato**, roughly
chopped
½ teaspoon mixed **dried herbs**
5 oz package **mozzarella
cheese**, drained and cubed

Make up the pizza dough according to package
instructions and turn out onto a lightly floured surface.
Divide the dough into 8 pieces. Knead each lightly to
produce smooth rounds, then roll into an 8 inch circle.
Loosely cover with plastic wrap.

Heat the oil in a large, nonstick skillet and cook the
peppers over a moderate heat for 5 minutes, stirring
occasionally. Add the chorizo slices and cook for
2 minutes before adding the tomato. Cook for an
additional 3–4 minutes, stirring occasionally, until the
tomato has softened. Remove from the heat and stir
in the herbs and mozzarella.

Allow to cool slightly before dividing the filling between
the 8 dough circles. Lightly brush the edges with a little
water, then fold the circles in half to enclose the filling
and press to seal. Place on a baking sheet and bake
in a preheated oven, 425°F, for 15–20 minutes.
Serve warm.

For butternut squash & feta cheese calzones,
heat 1 tablespoon olive oil in a pan and cook
8 oz cubed butternut squash over a moderate
heat for 5–6 minutes until beginning to soften. Add
5 tablespoons water, cover, and cook over a gentle
heat for 3 minutes. Remove from the heat and allow
to cool. Add 2 tablespoons chopped parsley and
4 oz crumbled feta. Use the filling as above.

mini scone pizzas

Serves **4**
Preparation time **25 minutes**
Cooking time **15–20 minutes**

1⅔ cups **self-rising whole-wheat flour**
¼ cup **butter**, cubed
⅔ cup **milk**
⅔ cup **passata (sieved tomatoes)**
3 tablespoons **tomato paste**
2 tablespoons chopped **basil**
4 thick slices good-quality **ham**, shredded
⅔ cup **pitted black olives**, halved
5 oz **mozzarella cheese**, grated

Sift the flour into a bowl and blend in the butter until the mixture resembles fine bread crumbs. Make a well in the center and stir in enough of the milk to give a fairly soft dough. Turn it out onto a lightly floured surface and knead gently. Cut into 4 pieces, then knead again to shape each into a rough round. Roll out 4 rough circles each to about 6 inches and place on a baking sheet.

Mix together the passata, tomato paste, and basil. Divide between the scone bases and spread to within ½ inch of the edges. Pile each with the ham and olives, then sprinkle with the mozzarella.

Drizzle with a little oil and bake in a preheated oven, 400°F, for 15–20 minutes until the bases are risen and the cheese is golden. Wrap in foil and serve warm or cold.

For egg & bacon scone pizzas, form each pizza base into a slight bowl shape with a ridge around the edge. Spread with the tomato sauce. Heat 1 tablespoon olive oil and cook 6 roughly chopped Canadian bacon slices for 2 minutes until golden. Drain on paper towels. Sprinkle the pizzas with the bacon pieces, then crack an egg over the top of each. Bake in the oven as above without the cheese. Remove from the oven and, while still warm, sprinkle each with 1 tablespoon grated mozzarella and some chopped parsley.

vegetable burgers

Serves **8**

Preparation time **20 minutes**, plus chilling

Cooking time **12–15 minutes**

5 cups **spinach**, washed and patted dry

1 tablespoon **olive oil**

1 small **red bell pepper**, cored, seeded, and very finely chopped

4 **scallions**, finely sliced

13 oz can **chickpeas**, drained and rinsed

½ cup **ricotta cheese**

1 **egg yolk**

½ teaspoon **ground coriander**

½ cup **all-purpose flour**

1 **egg**, beaten

3 cups **whole-wheat bread crumbs**

4 tablespoons **vegetable oil**

To serve

8 mini **burger buns**

tomato ketchup (optional, see pages 26–27)

cherry tomatoes (optional)

Put the moist spinach in a pan over a moderate heat for 2–3 minutes, stirring continuously, until wilted. Remove from the heat, drain well, and set aside.

Heat the olive oil in a skillet and cook the pepper and scallions over a moderate heat for 4–5 minutes until soft. Set aside.

Place the chickpeas in a food processor with the ricotta and blend until smooth. Add the spinach, egg yolk, and coriander and blend again to mix well. Transfer to a mixing bowl and fold in the pepper and scallion mixture. Shape the mixture into 8 patties, toss them lightly in the flour, then roll first in the beaten egg and then in the bread crumbs, to coat. Chill for 30 minutes.

Heat the vegetable oil in a large, heavy skillet and cook the burgers over a moderate heat for 6–7 minutes, turning once, until golden and crisp. Serve in the buns with tomato ketchup and cherry tomatoes, if desired.

For sausage & pepper burgers, cook the spinach, peppers, and onions as above. Chop the spinach roughly. Place 12 oz good-quality sausagemeat in a bowl and add 1 tablespoon tomato chutney and 1 teaspoon Dijon mustard. Mix well, then stir in the spinach, peppers, and onions and mix well. Do not coat, but simply heat the oil and cook for 2–3 minutes on each side until golden. Serve as above.

multicolored root fries

Serves **4**

Preparation time **15 minutes**

Cooking time **25–30 minutes**

2 **sweet potatoes**, cut into slim wedges with skin on

1 large **baking potato**, cut into slim wedges with skin on

2 **parsnips**, cut into long wedges

3 tablespoons **olive oil**

1 teaspoon **Cajun seasoning**

3 tablespoons chopped **parsley**

Mayonnaise

1 **egg**

⅔ cup **olive oil**

½ teaspoon **powdered mustard**

1 tablespoon **white wine vinegar**

1 tablespoon chopped **parsley**

Put the sweet potato, baking potato, and parsnip wedges in a bowl and drizzle with the olive oil, tossing well to coat lightly. Sprinkle with the Cajun seasoning and toss again to coat. Transfer to a large baking sheet and roast in a preheated oven, 400°F, for 25–30 minutes, until the vegetables are crisp and golden.

Meanwhile, make the mayonnaise. Place all the ingredients except the parsley in a small measuring cup, and using an electric blender whiz until a thick mayonnaise is formed. Stir in the parsley.

Serve the fries tossed with the parsley, with a tub of the mayonnaise to dip.

For cheese & chive mayonnaise to serve as an alternative accompaniment, make the mayonnaise as above and stir in 2 tablespoons sour cream, 1 tablespoon freshly grated Parmesan cheese, and 2 tablespoons fresh snipped chives. Serve with the root fries, to dip.

crispy lamb moroccan rolls

Serves **2**
Preparation time **15 minutes**
Cooking time **10 minutes**

8 oz **ground lamb**
1 teaspoon **ground cinnamon**
3 tablespoons **pine nuts**
2 **naan breads**, warmed
7 oz **hummus**
2 tablespoons **mint leaves**
1 small **crisphead lettuce**,
   finely shredded (optional)

Fry the lamb in a large, nonstick skillet for 8–10 minutes until it becomes golden brown. Add the cinnamon and pine nuts and cook again for 1 minute. Remove from the heat.

Place the warm naan breads on a cutting board and, using a rolling pin, firmly roll to flatten.

Mix the hummus with half the mint leaves, then spread in a thick layer over the warmed naans. Spoon over the crispy lamb, then sprinkle with the shredded lettuce, if using, and the remaining mint leaves. Tightly roll up and secure with toothpicks. Serve immediately, or wrap tightly in foil to transport.

For lamb kofta, mix the raw lamb with 4 finely chopped scallions, 1 teaspoon ground cinnamon, a very finely chopped tomato, and 1 egg yolk until blended together. Form into a very large, thin patty shape, and broil or cook in a large, heavy skillet on one side for 3 minutes, then on the other side for 2 minutes, until golden. Spread 1 warm naan with 2 tablespoons thick yogurt, sprinkle with the mint leaves and shredded lettuce, if using, and slip the large flattened kofta on top. Roll tightly and secure with toothpicks. Cut the kofta in half to serve 2.

chickpea & herb salad

Serves **4**

Preparation time **10 minutes**

Cooking time **5 minutes**
  (optional)

½ cup **bulghur wheat**

4 tablespoons **olive oil**

1 tablespoon **lemon juice**

2 tablespoons chopped **flat
  leaf parsley**

1 tablespoon chopped **mint**

13 oz can **chickpeas**, drained
  and rinsed

8 **cherry tomatoes**, halved

1 tablespoon chopped mild
  onion

½ cup diced **cucumber**

5 oz **feta cheese**, diced

Put the bulghur wheat in a heatproof bowl and pour over sufficient boiling water just to cover. Set aside until the water has been absorbed. (If you want to give a fluffier finish to the bulghur wheat, transfer it to a steamer and steam for 5 minutes. Spread out on a plate to cool.)

Mix together the oil, lemon juice, parsley, and mint in a large bowl. Add the chickpeas, tomatoes, onion, cucumber, and bulghur wheat. Mix well and add the feta, stirring lightly to avoid breaking up the cheese.

Serve immediately, or pack into an airtight container to transport.

For tuna, bean, & black olive salad, replace the chickpeas, tomatoes, onion, and cucumber with 1 x 7 oz can tuna, drained and flaked, 1 x 13 oz can mixed beans, drained and rinsed, ⅔ cup black olives, and 4 tablespoons lemon juice. Toss well before serving.

corn fritters & tomato dip

Makes **20**
Preparation time **15 minutes**
Cooking time **20–30 minutes**

¾ cup **all-purpose flour**
½ teaspoon **paprika**
⅔ cup **milk**
1 **egg**, beaten
9 oz can **corn**, drained
3 tablespoons chopped
   parsley
2 **scallions**, finely chopped
½ **red bell pepper**, finely
   chopped

Tomato dip
1 tablespoon **olive oil**
6 ripe **tomatoes**, roughly
   chopped
1 tablespoon **brown sugar**
½ teaspoon **paprika**
1 tablespoon **red wine**
   vinegar
4 tablespoons **vegetable oil**

Sift the flour and paprika into a bowl, then add the milk and egg and beat together to form a thick batter. Add the corn, parsley, scallions, and red pepper and mix well. If the mixture is too thick, add 1 tablespoon water to loosen. Set aside while making the tomato dip.

Heat the oil in a medium heavy pan, add the tomatoes, and cook over a moderate heat for 5 minutes, stirring occasionally. Add the sugar, paprika, and vinegar, reduce the heat, cover, and simmer over a very gentle heat for 10–15 minutes, stirring occasionally until the tomatoes are thick and pulpy. Remove from the heat and transfer to a bowl to cool.

Heat the vegetable oil in a large, nonstick skillet and spoon tablespoons of the corn mixture into the pan, well spaced apart, and cook for 1–2 minutes on each side, in batches, until golden and firm. Remove the fritters from the pan using a spatula and drain on paper towels.

Serve the corn fritters with a pot of the sauce, to dip, or wrap in foil to keep warm for transport.

For minted zucchini fritters, replace the corn with 1 finely chopped large zucchini. Heat 1 teaspoon of oil in a large skillet and cook the zucchini over a moderate heat for 3–4 minutes, stirring occasionally until pale golden. Add to the batter with 2 tablespoons of chopped mint.

chicken & bacon wraps

Serves **2**
Preparation time **15 minutes**
Cooking time **5 minutes**

1 tablespoon **olive oil**
2 x 5 oz boneless, skinless
  chicken breasts
2 **Canadian bacon** slices
2 **soft flour tortillas**
4 tablespoons **mayonnaise**
2 handfuls **spinach**

Lightly oil 2 sheets of plastic wrap with the oil. Place the 2 chicken breasts, well spaced apart, between the 2 sheets and bash with a rolling pin until the chicken is ¼ inch thick.

Heat a griddle or heavy skillet and cook the chicken for 5 minutes, turning once, until golden and cooked through, adding the bacon to the pan for the final 2 minutes.

Spread the tortillas each with 2 tablespoons mayonnaise. Place the chicken breast over the top, then lay 2 bacon slices on top of the chicken. Sprinkle with the spinach, then roll up tightly, securing with toothpicks. Cut in half and serve immediately, or wrap tightly in waxed paper and secure with string to transport.

For tuna & coleslaw wraps, drain a 7 oz can of tuna in brine, and mix with 2 roughly chopped tomatoes and 1 tablespoon chopped chives. Mix ⅛ cabbage, finely shredded, with 1 large grated carrot and 1 teaspoon poppy seeds and set aside. Mix 4 tablespoons mayonnaise with 2 tablespoons water until well blended, then pour over the cabbage and carrot and toss to mix. Spread the tuna mixture over 4 flour tortillas, then spoon over the coleslaw. Roll tightly and secure with toothpicks as above.

green bean & bacon frittata

Serves **4**
Preparation time **10 minutes**
Cooking time **about 10 minutes**

1½ cups **green beans**
6 **Canadian bacon** slices
⅔ cup frozen **peas**, defrosted
6 **eggs**
1 teaspoon **wholegrain mustard**
½ teaspoon **ground paprika**
2 tablespoons **vegetable oil**
4 tablespoons freshly grated **Parmesan cheese**

Cook the green beans in boiling water for 5 minutes. Drain and refresh with cold water to stop them from cooking more, then roughly chop and set aside. Meanwhile, place the bacon under a preheated medium broiler for 3–4 minutes until golden and cooked. Cool slightly, then snip roughly with scissors. Toss the green beans and bacon with the peas.

Beat the eggs with the mustard and paprika. Heat the oil in a medium nonstick skillet with a metal handle, then pour in the eggs. Working quickly, sprinkle over the beans, peas, and bacon. Cook over a gentle heat until the base has set.

Sprinkle with the Parmesan and place the pan under the broiler for 2–3 minutes until the frittata is set and golden.

Cut the frittata into wedges. If not serving immediately, wrap it in foil to keep warm.

For mushroom & bacon frittata, omit the beans and peas. Heat 1 tablespoon olive oil in a skillet and cook 8 oz quartered chestnut mushrooms for 4–5 minutes until soft and golden. Pour into the egg mixture in the pan and cook as above, with the Parmesan sprinkled over before broiling. Serve cut into wedges, either warm or cold.

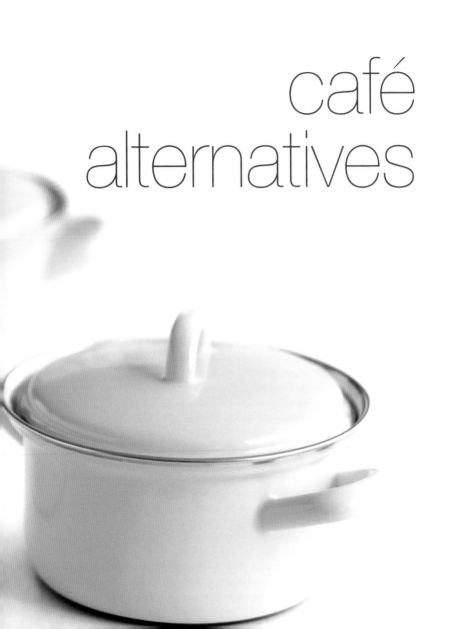

café
alternatives

lightly spiced chicken nuggets

Serves **4**
Preparation time **15 minutes**
Cooking time **15–20 minutes**

½ cup **all-purpose flour**
4 x 5 oz boneless, skinless
  chicken breasts, cut into
  bite-size chunks
1 **egg**, beaten
3 cups **fine whole-wheat
  bread crumbs**
1 teaspoon **Cajun spice**
2 tablespoons chopped
  parsley
Tomato Ketchup (see pages
  26–27), to dip

Place the flour on a plate and toss the chicken in it.

Pour the beaten egg onto a plate. Mix the bread crumbs with the Cajun spice and parsley on a separate plate. Dip each of the chicken pieces in the beaten egg, then toss in the seasoned bread crumbs, and place on a large baking sheet.

Bake the chicken nuggets in a preheated oven, 400°F, for 15–20 minutes until golden and cooked through.

Serve hot with tomato ketchup to dip, if desired.

For salmon goujons, replace the chicken with salmon fillets. Cut the fillets into chunks or strips and toss in bread crumbs seasoned with the finely grated zest of 1 lemon, instead of Cajun spice, and the parsley as above. Bake for 10–15 minutes and serve with mayonnaise flavored with the juice from the lemon.

ham & fresh pineapple pizza

Serves **4**

Preparation time **25 minutes**, plus rising

Cooking time **about 20 minutes**

1⅔ cups **whole-wheat all-purpose flour**

½ teaspoon **salt**

1 teaspoon instant **dried yeast**

⅔ cup warm **water**

1 tablespoon **olive oil**, plus extra for oiling

Topping

2 tablespoons **olive oil**

1 small **onion**, finely chopped

⅔ cup **passata (sieved tomatoes)**

3 tablespoons **tomato paste**

3 slices good-quality, thick **ham**, cut into strips

2 thick rings of fresh

5 oz **mozzarella cheese**, thinly sliced

thyme leaves, to garnish (optional)

Sift the flour and salt into a bowl, add the yeast and mix well. Make a well in the center and add the measured water and oil. Stir until it forms a wet dough, then beat for 2 minutes. Turn the dough out onto a well floured surface and knead for about 2 minutes until it becomes smooth and elastic. Roll out to a 12 inch circle, and place on a lightly oiled baking sheet. Cover with lightly oiled plastic wrap and leave in a warm place while making the topping.

Heat 1 tablespoon of the oil in a small skillet and cook the onion over a moderate heat for 2–3 minutes. Remove from the heat and add the passata and tomato paste. Spread over the pizza base to within 1 inch of the edges, and sprinkle with the ham.

Toss the pineapple with the remaining oil. Sprinkle it over the ham, then top with the mozzarella. Bake in a preheated oven, 425°F, for 15–18 minutes until golden. Sprinkle with thyme leaves, if desired.

For chicken & chorizo pizza, replace the ham and pineapple with 2 x 5 oz boneless, skinless chicken breasts and 4 oz chorizo sausage, both thinly sliced. Heat 1 tablespoon olive oil in a skillet and cook the chicken over a moderate heat for 3–4 minutes until golden. Add the chorizo and fry for 1 minute more. Toss with 3 tablespoons fresh basil and pile onto the pizza base, then top with the mozzarella. Omit the thyme.

chicken satay skewers

Serves **4**
Preparation time **20 minutes**,
  plus marinating
Cooking time **8–10 minutes**

6 tablespoons **dark soy sauce**
2 tablespoons **sesame oil**
1 teaspoon **Chinese 5-spice
  powder**
12 oz boneless, skinless
  chicken breasts, cut into
  long, thin strips

Sauce
4 tablespoons **peanut butter**
1 tablespoon **dark soy sauce**
½ teaspoon **ground coriander**
½ teaspoon **ground cumin**
pinch of **paprika** or **chili
  powder**
8 tablespoons **water**
cucumber, cut into strips,
  to serve

Place the soy sauce, sesame oil, and 5-spice powder into a bowl and mix. Add the chicken and toss together to coat in the marinade. Cover and set aside for 1 hour, stirring occasionally.

Thread the chicken, zigzag fashion, onto 10 soaked bamboo skewers (soaking them in warm water for 30 minutes will prevent the sticks burning while cooking), and place the chicken under a hot broiler for 8–10 minutes, turning once, until golden and cooked through.

Meanwhile, put all the sauce ingredients in a small pan and heat, stirring, until warm and well mixed. Transfer to a small serving bowl.

Place the bowl of sauce on a serving plate with the cucumber on one side and the hot chicken skewers around it.

For pork satay skewers, replace the chicken with 12 oz pork tenderloin, cut into long strips along its length. Complete and cook as above. For children who can handle a hotter sauce, fry ½ small red chili, finely chopped, in 1 teaspoon cooking oil and add to the peanut sauce.

mini steak burgers

Makes **8**
Preparation time **10 minutes**,
plus chilling
Cooking time **12–15 minutes**

12 oz **fine ground steak**
2 tablespoons **tomato
ketchup**
1 tablespoon **wholegrain
mustard**
3 tablespoons chopped
chives
1 tablespoon **olive oil**
4 oz **chestnut mushrooms**,
sliced
8 thin slices **Gruyère cheese**

To serve
4 **mini burger buns**, cut in half
ketchup or **sauces**

Place the steak in a bowl with the ketchup, mustard,
and chives. Mix really well together, working the mixture
with a fork to grind and blend the ingredients. Shape
into 8 patties and place on a plate. Cover with plastic
wrap and chill for 30 minutes to firm.

Heat the oil in a large skillet or griddle pan and cook
the mushrooms over a high heat for 3–4 minutes until
golden and soft. Remove from the pan using a slotted
spoon. Add the burgers and cook over a moderate heat
for 4–5 minutes on each side until golden and cooked
through. Sit a Gruyère slice on top of each of the
burgers and cover with a baking sheet for 1 minute
to allow the cheese to soften.

Top the base of each bun with a burger, then spoon
over the mushrooms and spread the top half of each
bun with ketchup or a sauce of the child's choice.
Place the lids on, and serve.

For pork & apple burgers, replace the ground steak
with 12 oz good-quality ground pork. Core 1 dessert
apple and grate with the skin on. Add to the mince
with the mustard and chives and blend well together
using a fork. Form into 8 patties, and cook as above.

sweet & sour pork noodles

Serves **4**
Preparation time **15 minutes**
Cooking time **12–16 minutes**

8 tablespoons **tomato ketchup**
3 tablespoons **brown sugar**
2 tablespoons **white wine vinegar**
6 oz medium **egg noodles**
2 tablespoons **sesame oil**
12 oz lean **pork**, cut into strips
1 inch piece fresh **ginger root**, peeled and chopped
1 **garlic clove**, crushed
1 cup **snow peas**, halved in length
1 large **carrot**, cut into strips
1¾ cups **bean sprouts**
7 oz can **bamboo shoots**, drained

Place the ketchup, sugar, and vinegar in a small saucepan and heat gently for 2–3 minutes until the sugar has dissolved, then set aside.

Cook the egg noodles for 3–5 minutes or according to package instructions until tender, then drain and set aside.

Heat the oil in a wok or large, heavy skillet and cook the pork strips over a high heat for 2–3 minutes until beginning to turn golden, then add the ginger, garlic, snow peas, and carrot. Stir-fry for an additional 2 minutes, then add the bean sprouts and bamboo shoots and stir-fry for 1 minute until all the ingredients are piping hot.

Add the warm, drained noodles and sauce and toss over the heat, using 2 spoons to mix really well, and heat through. Serve in warmed serving bowls.

For shrimp stir-fry with a thickened soy sauce, heat the oil and cook the ginger, garlic, snow peas, and carrot for 2–3 minutes, then add the bean sprouts and bamboo shoots and 8 oz shrimp and stir-fry for 1–2 minutes. Replace the sauce ingredients with ⅔ cup soy sauce, gently heated in a small pan. Add 1 tablespoon cornstarch blended with 2 tablespoons water and ½ teaspoon Chinese 5-spice powder. Stir until warmed and thickened, then remove from the heat. Add to the stir-fry, toss, and serve.

shrimp toasts

Serves **4**
Preparation time **15 minutes**
Cooking time **about
5 minutes**

6 oz **shrimp**
1 inch piece fresh **ginger
root**, peeled and finely
grated
1 **scallion**, finely chopped
1 **egg white**, beaten
1 tablespoon **cornstarch**
1 teaspoon **sesame oil**
1 teaspoon **dark soy sauce**,
plus extra to serve
4 medium-cut slices **bread**
4 tablespoons **sesame seeds**
6 tablespoons **vegetable oil**

Place the shrimp in a food processor with the ginger,
scallion, egg white, cornstarch, sesame oil, and soy
sauce and whiz to form a thick paste.

Spread the mixture on each of the slices of bread. Place
the sesame seeds on a large plate and press the shrimp
toast, shrimp side down, in the seeds to lightly cover.

Heat 2 tablespoons of the oil in a large, heavy skillet.
Cook 2 of the shrimp toasts, shrimp side down first
for 1–2 minutes until golden; then turn over and cook
the other side for 1 minute until golden. Repeat the
process wiping out the pan with paper towels and
heating the remaining oil first. Drain on paper towels,
then cut into triangles.

Serve the toasts with plenty of cucumber and corn
salsa (see below), if desired.

For cucumber & corn salsa to serve as an
accompaniment, finely chop ¼ cucumber and place
in a bowl with 4 tablespoons chopped fresh cilantro
and a 7 oz can corn, drained. Finely chop ½ red bell
pepper and add to the mix, then add 1 tablespoon
sweet chili sauce and mix together. Spoon onto the
sesame shrimp toasts to serve.

fish & chips in paper cones

Serves **4**
Preparation time **20 minutes**
Cooking time **30–40 minutes**

1 ½ lb **baking potatoes**, cut
   into thick fries
2 tablespoons **olive oil**
2 ½ cups **whole-wheat bread
   crumbs**
finely grated zest of 1 **lemon**
3 tablespoons chopped
   parsley
4 x 5 oz chunky **white fish
   fillets**, each cut into
   4 chunky pieces or goujons
½ cup **all-purpose flour**
1 **egg**, beaten
Tomato Ketchup (see pages
   26–27), to serve

Toss the potato fries with the oil, then roast in a preheated oven, 400°F, for 30–40 minutes, turning occasionally until golden and crisp.

Meanwhile, toss the bread crumbs with the lemon zest and parsley on a plate. Lightly coat the fish goujons in the flour, then the beaten egg, and finally the bread crumbs. Place on a baking sheet and roast in a preheated oven, 400°F, for the final 20 minutes of the fries' cooking time, until the fish is opaque and cooked through.

Roll 4 small sheets of paper into cones and seal with tape. Place in a bottle holder to help load each with fries, and place 4 goujons on top. Allow the kids to eat these healthy fish and chips with their fingers, dipping them into the ketchup for good measure!

For lemony mayonnaise dip to serve as an alternative accompaniment, place 1 egg, ⅔ cup olive oil, and 1 tablespoon white wine vinegar in a bowl and whiz with a hand blender until a thick mayonnaise is formed. Fold in the grated zest of 1 small lemon and 2 tablespoons of the juice, along with 2 tablespoons chopped parsley.

chicken fajitas & no-chili salsa

Serves **4**
Preparation time **20 minutes**
Cooking time **about 5 minutes**

½ teaspoon **ground coriander**
½ teaspoon **ground cumin**
½ teaspoon **ground paprika**
1 **garlic clove**, crushed
3 tablespoons chopped
  cilantro
12 oz boneless, skinless
  chicken breasts, cut into
  bite-size strips
1 tablespoon **olive oil**
4 **soft flour tortillas**
sour cream, to serve
  (optional)

Salsa

3 large, ripe **tomatoes**, finely
  chopped
3 tablespoons chopped
  cilantro
⅛ **cucumber**, finely chopped
1 tablespoon **olive oil**

Guacamole

1 large **avocado**, roughly
  chopped
grated zest and juice of ½ **lime**
2 teaspoons **sweet chili**
  sauce (optional)

Place all the ground spices, garlic, and cilantro in a mixing bowl. Toss the chicken in the oil, then add to the spices and toss to coat lightly in the spice mixture.

Make the salsa, mix the tomatoes, cilantro, and cucumber in a bowl and drizzle over the oil. Transfer to a serving bowl.

Make the guacamole, mash the avocado with the lime zest and juice and sweet chili sauce, if using, until soft and rough-textured. Transfer to a serving bowl.

Heat a griddle pan or heavy skillet and cook the chicken for 3–4 minutes, turning occasionally, until golden and cooked through. Fill the tortillas with the hot chicken slices, guacamole, and salsa, and fold into quarters. Spoon over a little sour cream, if desired.

For beef fajitas, replace the chicken with sirloin steak, cut into bite-size strips. For a slightly "warmer" version, replace the paprika with mild chili powder.

cheese & bacon pastries

Serves **6**
Preparation time **15 minutes**
Cooking time **20–25 minutes**

1 lb package **puff pastry**
flour, for dusting
2 teaspoons **Dijon mustard**
(optional)
2 oz **Gruyère cheese**, thinly
sliced
2 oz **cheddar cheese**, thinly
sliced
3 tablespoons chopped
parsley
6 **Canadian bacon** slices,
thinly sliced
beaten **egg**

Roll out the pastry on a lightly floured surface to a
rectangle measuring 12 x 18 inches. Cut the pastry
into 6 inch squares.

Spread the pastry all over with a thin layer of mustard.
Arrange the Gruyère and cheddar slices on each of
the pastry squares in a diagonal line. Sprinkle with the
parsley, then ruffle the bacon across the top. Lightly
brush the pastry edges with a little warm water, then
fold each of the opposite corners up and over the
filling to meet, then press to seal with a fork. Place
on a baking sheet.

Lightly brush the pastries with beaten egg and bake
in a preheated oven, 400°F, for 20–25 minutes until
golden. Serve warm.

For haloumi & tomato pastries, replace the bacon
and cheeses with 6 oz haloumi cheese, thinly sliced,
and 6 halved cherry tomatoes. Arrange on top of the
mustard-spread pastry and sprinkle with the parsley.
Bake as above until golden.

super snacks

banana & raisin squares

Makes **12**
Preparation time **10 minutes**
Cooking time **10 minutes**

⅔ cup **butter**
⅔ cup **maple syrup**
⅔ cup **raisins**
2 large **bananas**, well mashed
3¾ cups **rolled oats**

Place the butter in a medium pan with the maple syrup and melt over a gentle heat. Stir in the raisins. Remove from the heat and add the bananas, stirring well. Add the oats and stir well until all the oats have been coated.

Spoon the mixture into an 11 x 7 inch nonstick jelly roll pan and level the surface using a potato masher for ease. Bake in a preheated oven, 375°F, for 10 minutes until the top is just beginning to turn a pale golden. The mixture will still seem somewhat soft.

Allow to cool for 10 minutes in the pan before cutting into 12 squares. Remove from the pan and allow to cool completely.

For ginger squares, add 1 teaspoon ground ginger to the melted butter and maple syrup and replace the bananas with 4 pieces stem ginger, finely chopped. Stir through with the raisins and spoon into the prepared pan and level. Bake and cut into squares as above.

bread monsters

Makes **8**

Preparation time **30 minutes**, plus rising

Cooking time **15–20 minutes**

2¼ cups **bread flour**, plus extra for dusting

1 teaspoon **salt**

⅛ oz instant **dried yeast**

1 tablespoon **vegetable oil**

¾ cup **warm water**

12 **currants**, cut in half, for the eyes and mouths

1 **egg**, beaten

Sift the flour and salt together in a mixing bowl and add the yeast, oil, and water. Mix everything together with a wooden spoon, then use your hands to draw the mixture together into a firm dough. If the mixture is too dry to come together, add a little more water. If the mixture sticks to your hands, add some more flour.

Turn the dough out onto a well-floured surface and knead thoroughly for at least 5 minutes, then divide it into 8 equal pieces and knead into balls. Make a pointy snout at one end of each ball and place on a baking sheet lined with nonstick parchment paper. Leave plenty of space between the rolls as they will double in size. Make prickles on the monsters by snipping into the dough with the tips of scissors. Press the currant halves into the dough to make the eyes and mouths.

Cover the rolls with a clean dish towel, then leave in a warm place for 1 hour or until they have doubled in size.

Brush the rolls with the beaten egg and bake in a preheated oven, 450°F, for 15–20 minutes. If the rolls are cooked, they will sound hollow when tapped on the bottom (remember to pick them up with an oven mitt as they will be hot). Transfer to a wire rack to cool.

For sweet bread roll snacks, add 1½ cups mixed dried fruit to the dry ingredients with 2 teaspoons ground cinnamon and 3 tablespoons superfine sugar. Continue as above, shaping into 8 round balls and baking as above. Cool and serve either warm or cold, split and spread thinly with a little unsalted butter.

a very happy birthday cake

Serves **12**
Preparation time **25 minutes**
Cooking time **35–40 minutes**

¾ cup **soft margarine**, plus
  extra for greasing
¾ cup **superfine sugar**
2 teaspoons **vanilla extract**
2½ cups **self-rising flour**
2 teaspoons **baking powder**
3 **eggs**
¼ cup **ground rice**
⅔ cup **low-fat plain yogurt**
1 cup **strawberries**, finely
  chopped, plus extra to
  decorate
1¼ cups **heavy cream**
3 tablespoons **reduced-sugar
  strawberry jelly**

Grease 2 x 8 inch removable-bottomed, round cake pans lightly with margarine, and line the bases of the pans with nonstick parchment paper. Cream the margarine and sugar in a food processor with the vanilla extract until smooth.

Sift the flour and baking powder over the creamed mixture, add the eggs, ground rice, and yogurt and whiz together until creamy. Fold one-third of the strawberries into the mixture.

Divide the mixture between the prepared pans and bake in a preheated oven, 350°F, for 35–40 minutes until risen, golden, and springy to the touch. Allow to cool in the pans for 10 minutes before removing to a wire rack to cool completely. Remove the parchment paper.

Beat the cream until soft peaks form. Cut the top off one of the cakes to level it, then spread with the jelly and then half of the cream to the edges. Sprinkle with two-thirds of the strawberries. Place the other cake on top and spread with the remaining cream. Decorate with the remaining strawberries or form them into your child's initials. Add candles.

For chocolate birthday cake, replace ¼ cup of the flour with cocoa powder and bake as above. Omit the jelly and simply fill with the cream. Replace the strawberries with 1 cup chocolate-coated honeycomb balls, lightly crushed and used to fill and decorate the cake.

rudolph's santa snacks

Makes **about 14**
Preparation time **15 minutes**
Cooking time **15 minutes**

2 cups **cornflakes**
½ cup **butter** or **margarine**,
   softened
⅓ cup **superfine sugar**
1 **egg yolk**
few drops **vanilla extract**
1 cup **self-rising flour**
3 tablespoons **cornstarch**
7 **candied cherries**, sliced in
   half, to decorate

Place the cornflakes in a plastic bag. Crush them with your hands or bash them with a rolling pin, then tip on to a plate and set aside.

Put the butter and sugar into a mixing bowl and cream them together with a wooden spoon until pale and fluffy. Add the egg yolk and vanilla extract and stir in. Sift in the flour and cornstarch and stir them into the mix.

Take walnut-size amounts of the mixture and make them into about 14 balls. Roll the balls in the crushed cornflakes until covered, then place them on a baking sheet lined with nonstick parchment paper, leaving plenty of space between them, and decorate the top of each one with half a candied cherry.

Bake the cookies in a preheated oven, 375°F, for 15 minutes, or until a light golden brown, then remove from the oven and allow to cool a little before transferring to a wire cooling rack.

For Santa's chocolate snowy snacks, add ⅓ cup semisweet chocolate drops to the mixture with the flour and cornstarch, then add 1 tablespoon cocoa powder. Stir and then cook as above. Once cooked, dust with a little confectioners' sugar to resemble snow.

melon & pineapple salad

Serves **4**
Preparation time **10 minutes**

½ **cantaloupe melon**, peeled,
seeded, and diced
½ small **pineapple**, peeled
and diced
finely grated zest of 1 **lime**
2 teaspoons **fructose**
quarter slices of **lime**, to
decorate

Put the melon and pineapple in a bowl or plastic
storage box.

Mix together the lime zest and fructose until well
combined. Sprinkle over the fruit and mix together
well—in 1 hour or so the fructose will have dissolved.

Decorate with the lime slices and serve.

For watermelon, pear, & strawberry salad, cut
½ small watermelon into cubes and place in a plastic
storage box. Toss with 2 peeled, cored, and sliced
pears and 1 cup hulled and halved small strawberries.
Mix with 3 tablespoons orange juice and decorate
with orange or clementine slices.

blueberry & cream cheese traybake

Serves **12**
Preparation time **20 minutes**
Cooking time **20 minutes**

¾ cup **butter**, softened
⅓ cup **brown sugar**
1½ cups **cream cheese**
2 teaspoons **vanilla extract**
3 **eggs**
1½ cups **all-purpose flour**
1¼ cups **whole-wheat flour**
1½ cups **blueberries**
¾ cup **confectioners' sugar**, sifted
½ teaspoon **ground cinnamon** (optional)

Grease an 11 x 7 inch deep jelly roll pan lightly with butter and line the base with nonstick parchment paper.

Place ⅔ cup of the butter into a bowl and beat well until smooth with a wooden spoon. Add the sugar, ⅔ cup of the cream cheese, and the vanilla extract and beat again. Add the eggs and sift in the flours. Mix together to combine well.

Fold the blueberries into the cake mixture, then transfer to the prepared pan and level. Bake in a preheated oven, 350°F, for 20 minutes until golden and firm to the touch. Allow to cool for 10 minutes in the pan before turning the cake out onto a wire rack to cool completely.

Beat together the remaining cream cheese and remaining butter with the confectioners' sugar and half of the cinnamon, if using, and spread over the surface of the cake. Cut into 12 squares, then sprinkle with the remaining cinnamon, if desired.

For raspberry & orange traybake, add the grated zest of ½ orange to the creamed butter, sugar, and cream cheese mixture, then replace the blueberries with 1 cup raspberries, folding in very carefully so as not to break up the fruit. Bake as above, then make up the same topping, replacing the cinnamon with the remaining orange zest, and spread over the top.

cheesy twists

Makes **about 15**
Preparation time **15 minutes**
Cooking time **8–12 minutes**

½ cup grated **cheddar cheese**
¾ cup **self-rising flour**, plus
  extra for dusting
½ teaspoon **powdered
  mustard**
¼ cup chilled **butter**, cut into
  cubes
1 **egg yolk**

Put the cheddar into a mixing bowl, then sift the flour and powdered mustard into the bowl. Add the butter, then blend the cheese, butter, and flour together until the butter is broken up and covered in flour and the mixture looks like fine bread crumbs. Add the egg yolk to the mixture and stir with a wooden spoon until you have a stiff dough.

Roll out the dough on a well-floured surface until it is about ¼ inch thick. Take a sharp knife and cut the dough into about 15 long strips, about ½ inch thick. Pick up each strip carefully and twist it gently before laying it on a baking sheet lined with nonstick parchment paper.

Bake the twists in a preheated oven, 425°F, for 8–12 minutes until golden brown, then remove them from the oven and allow to cool on the baking sheet.

For spinach & Parmesan twists, place the flour in a food processor with a handful of spinach leaves and whiz until fine and green in color. Add the remaining ingredients, replacing the cheddar with freshly grated Parmesan, then continue as above.

grandma's zucchini loaf

Serves **8–10**

Preparation time **30 minutes**

Cooking time **about 1 hour 15 minutes**

2¼ cups **self-rising flour**

1 teaspoon **baking powder**

2 teaspoons **mixed spice**

2 **zucchini**, grated

½ cup **brown sugar**

1 **egg**

5 tablespoons **milk**

⅓ cup **butter**, plus extra for greasing

½ cup **raisins**

⅔ cup **walnuts**, chopped

Topping

½ cup **all-purpose flour**

2 tablespoons **brown sugar**

½ teaspoon **mixed spice**

¼ cup chilled **butter**, cut into cubes

½ cup **walnuts**, finely chopped

Grease a 2 lb loaf pan lightly with butter and line the base with nonstick parchment paper. Sift the flour, baking powder, and mixed spice into a large bowl and add the zucchini and sugar. Stir well.

Beat the egg and milk together in a bowl. Melt the butter in a small pan, then add the raisins and stir well over a gentle heat for a few seconds to help plump them up. Pour the melted butter and milk and egg mixture into the dry ingredients and stir until well combined. Add the walnuts and stir again. Transfer to the prepared pan and level.

Make the streusel topping: mix the flour with the sugar and mixed spice, then blend the butter into the dry ingredients until the mixture resembles fine bread crumbs. Stir in the walnuts, then sprinkle over the cake.

Bake the loaf in a preheated oven, 350°F, for 1 hour to 1 hour 10 minutes until well risen and firm to the touch and a skewer inserted comes out clean. Allow it to cool for 10 minutes in the pan before turning out onto a wire rack to cool completely.

For moist mango loaf, replace the zucchini, raisins, and walnuts with ¾ cup mango puree, 1 teaspoon vanilla extract, and ½ mango, roughly chopped, all folded into the wet mixture. Use the same streusel topping as above, but bake for 40–45 minutes until firm and well risen.

berried treasures

Serves **4**

Preparation time **15 minutes**

Cooking time **2 minutes**

4 oz **white chocolate**, at room
   temperature

2 tablespoons **milk**

⅔ cup **heavy cream**

1 cup **blackberries**

1 tablespoon **honey**

1 **egg white**

Break off a quarter of the white chocolate. Using a potato peeler, shave off some chocolate curls to decorate the desserts.

Place the remaining pieces of chocolate in a small heatproof bowl. Add the milk and microwave on full power for 2 minutes. Allow to stand for 1 minute then stir. If lumps remain in the chocolate, microwave again for 30 seconds more until melted. (Alternatively, put the chocolate and milk in a small heatproof bowl and rest it over a small saucepan of gently simmering water.) Stir in the cream and pour into a cool bowl, allow to cool completely, then put in the freezer for 5 minutes.

Reserve 4 blackberries and blend the remainder in a food processor with the honey until pureed. Turn into a fine-meshed strainer over a bowl and press the puree through with the back of a dessertspoon to extract the seeds.

Beat the egg white until it stands in soft peaks when the beater is lifted from the bowl.

Remove the chocolate cream from the freezer and beat until it starts to thicken. This might take a few minutes. Gently stir in the egg white.

Spoon half the chocolate mixture into 4 small serving dishes or cups and spoon over the fruit puree. Top with the remaining chocolate mixture and give each a light stir with the handle end of a teaspoon so you can see a swirl of the blackberry puree. Decorate with the reserved berries and chocolate curls and chill until ready to serve.

granola squares

Makes **12**
Preparation time **15 minutes**,
    plus chilling
Cooking time **20 minutes**

¾ cup **butter**, plus extra for
    greasing
⅔ cup **honey**
2 tablespoons **maple syrup**
1 teaspoon **ground cinnamon**
¾ cup ready-to-eat **dried
    apricots**, roughly chopped
¾ cup ready-to-eat **dried
    papaya** or **mango**, roughly
    chopped
¾ cup **raisins**
4 tablespoons **pumpkin seeds**
2 tablespoons **sesame seeds**
3 tablespoons **sunflower
    seeds**
¾ cup **pecan nuts**, roughly
    chopped
2¾ cups **rolled oats**

Grease an 11 x 7 inch deep jelly roll pan with butter and line the base with nonstick parchment paper.

Place the butter, honey, and maple syrup in a medium saucepan and heat, stirring continually, until the butter has melted. Add the cinnamon, dried fruit, seeds, and nuts, stir the mixture, and heat for 1 minute. Remove from the heat and add the rolled oats, stirring until they are well coated in the syrup.

Transfer the mixture to the prepared pan and smooth down with the back of a spoon to compact into the pan and level. Bake in a preheated oven, 350°F, for 15 minutes until the top is just beginning to brown. Remove from the oven and allow to cool in the pan, then chill in the refrigerator for 30–60 minutes.

Turn out the chilled granola, upside down, on a cutting board, then carefully flip it back over to its correct side. Using a long, sharp knife (preferably longer than the granola itself), cut into 12 squares.

For fruity chocolate granola squares, leave out the pecans and seeds and replace with ¾ cup roughly chopped ready-to-eat dried apples. Once cooled, drizzle 2 oz melted white chocolate over the top. Allow to set in the refrigerator for 10 minutes before cutting into squares.

choc-peanut cake

Makes a **2 lb loaf cake**
Preparation time **15 minutes**
Cooking time **about 1 hour**

1 cup **all-purpse flour**
⅛ cup **whole-wheat flour**
1 teaspoon **baking powder**
3 tablespoons **superfine sugar**
½ cup **smooth peanut butter**
½ cup **butter**, softened
3 **eggs**, lightly beaten
1 teaspoon **vanilla extract**
3 tablespoons **apple juice**
⅔ cup **semisweet chocolate chips** or 4 oz **semisweet chocolate**, chopped
1 large **dessert apple**, peeled, cored, and chopped

Line a 2 lb loaf pan with nonstick parchment paper. Sift the flours and baking powder into a large bowl. Mix in the sugar, peanut butter, butter, eggs, vanilla extract, and apple juice. Stir through the chocolate chips and apple.

Spoon the mixture into the prepared pan and bake in a preheated oven, 350°F, for 1 hour. To see if it is cooked, insert a skewer in the center of the loaf—if it comes out clean it is done, but if cake mix is attached to the skewer it will need another 10 minutes.

Remove the cake from the oven and turn out onto a wire rack. Peel off the parchment paper and allow to cool. Serve cut into slices.

For honey cake, replace the peanut butter with ⅓ cup honey and omit the chocolate chips. Drizzle with 2 tablespoons honey before serving.

cherry, bran, & raisin muffins

Makes **12**
Preparation time **15 minutes**
Cooking time **20–25 minutes**

1⅛ cups **oat bran**
2 cups **self-rising flour**
1 teaspoon **baking powder**
1 teaspoon **baking soda**
1 teaspoon **ground cinnamon**
½ teaspoon **ground ginger**
½ cup **brown sugar**
1 **egg**
5 tablespoons **vegetable oil**
6 tablespoons **milk**
1 cup **cherries**, pitted and
  halved
¾ cup **raisins**

Topping
1 cup **mascarpone cheese**
2 tablespoons **confectioners'
  sugar**

To decorate
12 **cherries**
pinch of **ground cinnamon**
  (optional)

Place the oat bran in a bowl. Sift the flour, baking powder, baking soda, cinnamon, and ginger over the top and mix together. Add the sugar and stir well.

Mix together in a pitcher the egg, oil, and milk, then pour into the dry ingredients with the cherries and raisins and stir until just mixed. Line a 12-cup muffin pan with 12 paper muffin cups and divide the mixture between them. Bake in a preheated oven, 350°F, for 20–25 minutes until well risen and golden. Remove the muffins from the pan and place on a wire rack to cool.

Beat the mascarpone and confectioners' sugar in a bowl, then spoon and swirl on top of each cooled muffin. Decorate each with a cherry and a sprinkling of cinnamon, if desired.

For carrot-cake muffins, omit the oat bran and increase the flour to 2¼ cups. Add 1 teaspoon mixed spice. Replace the cherries with 2 grated carrots and add ¾ cup roughly chopped walnuts or pecans. Bake as above, then decorate with the same topping and a walnut half instead of a cherry.

chocolate-toffee popcorn

Makes about **6 oz**
Preparation time **15 minutes**
Cooking time **about**
  10 minutes

about 2 oz **milk chocolate**,
  broken into pieces
2 oz **firm toffees**
4 tablespoons **milk**
1 tablespoon **vegetable oil**
9 cups **popcorn kernels**

Place the chocolate pieces in a small heatproof bowl. Microwave on medium power for 1 minute. Allow to stand for 2 minutes, then microwave again for 30 seconds at a time until melted, stirring frequently to avoid lumps. (Alternatively, melt the chocolate carefully in a small heatproof bowl over a small saucepan of gently simmering water.)

Unwrap the toffees and put them in a plastic bag. Place on a cutting board and tap firmly with a rolling pin until the toffees have broken into small pieces. Tip the pieces into a small saucepan and add the milk. Cook on the lowest possible heat until the toffee has melted (this will take several minutes, depending on the firmness of the toffee). Remove from the heat.

Put the oil in a large saucepan with a tight-fitting lid and heat for 1 minute. Add the popcorn kernels and cover with the lid. Cook until the popping sound stops, then tip the corn out onto a large baking sheet or roasting pan and leave for 5 minutes.

Using a teaspoon, drizzle lines of the toffee sauce over the corn until lightly coated. Drizzle with lines of chocolate in the same way.

For golden-nugget popcorn, cook the popcorn kernels as above, but replace the remaining ingredients with 4 tablespoons light corn syrup heated in a small pan with 2 tablespoons butter until melted, then add ⅓ cup roughly chopped roasted cashews. Cool slightly then toss with the popcorn to coat lightly.

banana & chocolate loaf cake

Serves **8–10**
Preparation time **15 minutes**
Cooking time **55–60 minutes**

1 cup **butter**, softened, plus
   extra for greasing
½ cup **superfine sugar**
1 teaspoon **vanilla extract**
3 **eggs**, beaten
2½ cups **self-rising flour**
1 teaspoon **baking powder**
3 ripe **bananas**, mashed
2 tablespoons **milk**
6 oz **semisweet chocolate**,
   roughly chopped, or 1 cup
   chocolate chips

Grease a 2 lb loaf pan lightly with butter and line the base with nonstick parchment paper. Beat the butter, sugar, and vanilla extract together in a bowl until smooth and creamy. Add the eggs and sift over the flour and baking powder. Beat together until smooth and creamy.

Add the bananas, milk, and chopped chocolate and fold together until well mixed. Transfer the mixture to the prepared pan and bake in a preheated oven, 350°F, for 55–60 minutes until the cake is well risen and golden.

Cool the cake in the pan for 10 minutes before turning out onto a wire rack to cool completely. Serve cut into slices.

For double-chocolate no-wheat banana loaf,
replace the flour with 1¾ cups rice flour and add 4 tablespoons of cocoa powder when sifting into the bowl.

vanilla flowers

Makes **30**
Preparation time **30 minutes**
Cooking time **10–15 minutes**

1 cup **butter**, softened
few drops **vanilla extract**
½ cup **confectioners' sugar**
1½ cups **all-purpose flour**
⅓ cup **cornstarch**
cake decorations, to decorate

Place the butter and vanilla extract in a mixing bowl and sift in the confectioners' sugar. Cream the ingredients together with a wooden spoon. Sift in the flour and the cornstarch a little at a time and fold in with a metal spoon.

Spoon the mixture into a pastry bag, and pipe the mixture onto a baking sheet lined with nonstick parchment paper, making little flower shapes. To finish a flower, push the tip down into the piped flower as you stop squeezing. Press a decoration into the center of each one.

Bake the cookies in a preheated oven, 375°F, for 10–15 minutes or until they are a pale golden color. Remove from the oven and allow to cool for a few minutes on the baking sheet before transferring to a cooling rack.

For ginger flowers, mix 1 teaspoon ground allspice or mixed spice in with the cornstarch. Decorate the center of each with ¼ piece stem ginger before baking as above.

upside-down tarts

Serves **4**
Preparation time **10 minutes**
Cooking time **15–18 minutes**

2 tablespoons **unsalted butter**
2 tablespoons **light brown sugar**
½ cup **red currants**
2 ripe **pears**, peeled, cored, and cut into chunky pieces
½ x 12 oz pack **ready-rolled puff pastry**, thawed if frozen and removed from the refrigerator

Thinly slice the butter and divide it among 4 small heatproof ramekin dishes. Sprinkle with the sugar. If the red currants are still attached to their stalks, reserve 4 clusters for decoration and remove the rest from the stalks (the easiest way to do this is to run the currants between the prongs of a fork). Sprinkle several redcurrants into each dish, then add the pears.

Unroll the pastry and cut out rounds using a 4 inch cookie cutter. Lay the pastry rounds over the pears, tucking the edges down inside the dishes.

Place the dishes on a baking sheet and bake in a preheated oven, 425°F, for 15–18 minutes or until the pastry is well risen and pale golden. Using an oven mitt, remove the baking sheet from the oven and put it on a heatproof surface. Allow to cool slightly.

Loosen the edges of the pastry with a knife. Hold a ramekin dish with an oven mitt and invert a small serving plate on top. Carefully flip over the dish and plate so that the plate is the right way up. Lift off the dish to reveal the tart with its fruity topping. Repeat with the remaining tarts. Serve decorated with the remaining red currants.

For banana & maple syrup upside-down tarts, replace the red currants and pears with 2 thinly sliced bananas, placing them in the bases of each of the buttered ramekins and drizzling each with 1 tablespoon maple syrup. Top with the pastry and bake as above.

pumpkin seed & fruit bars

Makes **8**
Preparation time **15 minutes**,
   plus chilling
Cooking time **5 minutes**

½ cup **pumpkin seeds**
½ cup **dried soy beans**
½ cup **raisins**
½ cup ready-to-eat **dried
   apricots**, roughly chopped
½ cup **dried cranberries**
10 oz **semisweet chocolate**,
   broken into pieces

Lightly grease an 11 x 7 inch jelly roll pan and line the base with nonstick parchment paper. Put the seeds, soy beans, and all the fruit into a bowl.

Melt the chocolate (see page 180). Remove from the heat, pour over the seed and fruit mixture, and stir well to coat completely.

Transfer the mixture to the prepared pan and level with the back of a spoon to fill the pan evenly. Chill in the refrigerator for 1 hour until set and firm. Cut into 8 bars and keep refrigerated in an airtight container until ready to use.

For yogurt-coated bars, replace the semisweet chocolate with 7 oz white chocolate melted over simmering water. When melted, remove from the heat and add 2 tablespoons plain yogurt and ½ teaspoon vanilla extract. Stir well, then add to the dry ingredients and stir to coat. Transfer into the pan and chill as above.

christmas garlands

Makes **6**
Preparation time **30 minutes**
Cooking time **about
  15 minutes**

¼ cup **butter**
1¼ cups **all-purpose flour**
¼ cup **superfine sugar**, plus
  a little for sprinkling
finely grated zest of 1 small
  lemon
1 **egg**, beaten
pieces of **angelica and
  candied cherries**, to
  decorate

Put the butter in a bowl, sift in the flour, and blend together until the mixture resembles fine bread crumbs. Add the sugar and lemon zest and stir everything together with a wooden spoon. Add most of the egg and stir again until the mixture comes together, then use your hands to draw the dough together into a ball.

Pick off small pieces of dough and roll them into balls, each about the size of a cherry. Press 8 balls of the cookie dough together into a circle, then repeat to make 5 more garlands. Place small pieces of candied cherry or angelica between the balls.

Place the garlands on a baking sheet lined with nonstick parchment paper and bake in a preheated oven, 375°F, for about 15 minutes or until pale golden. Just before the end of the cooking time, brush with the remainder of the egg and sprinkle with superfine sugar, then return to the oven to finish cooking.

Remove from the oven and allow to cool a little before transferring to a cooling rack. Thread onto ribbons and use as decorations.

For Christmas trees, using 10 small balls of dough per tree, create Christmas tree shapes by starting with 1 as a top row, followed by 2, 3, and 4 on the bottom row. This will create a classic triangular Christmas tree shape. Decorate the trees with angelica and candied cherries and bake as above.

chocolate scribble cake

Makes **9 squares**
Preparation time **15 minutes**
Cooking time **20 minutes**

2 oz **semisweet chocolate**,
   broken into small pieces
¼ cup **butter** or **margarine**
2 **eggs**
⅔ cup **light brown sugar**
½ cup **self-rising flour**
icing decorator tubes, to
   decorate (optional)

Melt the chocolate together with the butter (see page 180).

Break the eggs into a mixing bowl, then add the sugar and sift in the flour. Stir them together vigorously.

Stir the melted chocolate and butter and carefully pour them into the mixing bowl. Stir the mixture until smooth, then pour into a shallow cake pan, 8 inches square, lined with nonstick parchment paper, using the spatula to scrape every last bit from the bowl. Place on the top shelf of a preheated oven, 350°F, for 20 minutes or until just firm when you touch it very gently in the middle.

Allow the cake to cool in the pan, then cut it into 9 pieces in the pan. Using the decorator tubes, decorate the squares with icing scribbles, if desired.

For pink coconut cake, make single-stage cake mix of 1 cup self-rising flour, ½ cup soft margarine, ½ cup superfine sugar, and 2 eggs; beat together until smooth and creamy then transfer to an 8 inch greased and base-lined square pan. Bake in the preheated oven as above for 20 minutes until golden and a skewer inserted comes out clean. Transfer to a wire rack to cool. Mix ¾ cup sifted confectioners' sugar with 1–2 teaspoons beet juice until smooth and blended. Spread thinly over the cake and scatter with 1 tablespoon shredded coconut. Cut into squares to serve.

desserts

multicolored fresh fruit popsicles

Serves **8**
Preparation time **20 minutes**,
  plus freezing
Cooking time **15 minutes**

2½ cups fresh **raspberries**
2 tablespoons **superfine
  sugar**
⅔ cup **water**, plus
  4 tablespoons
13 oz can **peaches** in
  natural juice

Place the raspberries and sugar in a small pan with 4 tablespoons of the measured water and bring to a boil, stirring well until the sugar dissolves. Add the remaining measured water.

Put the raspberry liquid through a sieve, pressing down well with a metal spoon to make as much of the pulp go through as possible, only discarding the seeds.

Pour the mixture into 8 popsicle molds, filling just the base of each. (Try using 8 rinsed yogurt cartons placed in a roasting pan. Cover with foil and push popsicle sticks through the foil into the center of each pot. The foil will help secure the stick in the center.) Freeze for 1–2 hours until firm.

Meanwhile, put the peaches and juice into a food processor and whiz until smooth. Once the raspberry base is firm, pour the peach liquid over the top of the raspberry mixture and freeze for an additional 1–2 hours or overnight until firm.

For yogurt peach melba popsicles, omit the sugar and water and whiz together the raspberries, peaches, and ⅔ cup raspberry-flavored drinking yogurt in a food processor. Divide between 8 popsicle molds and freeze for 4–5 hours until firm.

sugared fruit pancakes

Makes **20–24**
Preparation time **15 minutes**
Cooking time **10 minutes**

2 **eggs**
2 tablespoons **unsalted butter**
6 tablespoons **milk**
scant cup **all-purpose flour**
1 teaspoon **baking powder**
2 tablespoons **vanilla** or **superfine sugar**
1 cup **blueberries**
cooking oil, for frying

Separate the eggs into 2 bowls, egg yolks in one and egg whites in another. Put the butter in a heatproof bowl and heat in the microwave for 30 seconds until melted. Add the milk and pour the mixture over the egg yolks, stirring well.

Put the flour, baking powder, and 1 tablespoon of the sugar in a large bowl. Add the milk mixture and beat well to make a smooth batter. Stir in the blueberries.

Beat the egg whites until they form firm peaks. Using a large metal spoon, gently fold the whites into the batter until well mixed.

Heat a little oil in a large skillet for 1 minute. Add a dessertspoonful of the batter to one side of the pan so it spreads to make a little cake. Add 2–3 more spoonfuls, depending on the size of the pan, so the pancakes can cook without touching. When the pancakes are golden on the underside (check by lifting with a turner or spatula), flip them over and cook again until golden. Remove the pancakes from the pan and transfer to a serving plate, then keep them warm while you cook the remainder.

Sprinkle with the remaining sugar and serve.

For vanilla & fig pancakes, add 1 teaspoon vanilla extract to the milk in the pancakes, omit the blueberries and make as above. Cut 3 small figs into wedges and place into a pan with 1 tablespoon unsalted butter and 3 tablespoons maple syrup and heat for 2 minutes, stirring until soft. Spoon over the warm pancakes and serve with yogurt.

toffee peaches

Serves **4**
Preparation time **10 minutes**
Cooking time **15 minutes**

4 **peaches**, halved and pitted
½ cup **ground almonds**

Sauce
½ cup **light brown sugar**
5 tablespoons **maple syrup**
2 tablespoons **butter**
⅔ cup **light cream**

Cut 4 x 8 inch square pieces of foil and place 2 peach halves in each. Sprinkle with the ground almonds. Scrunch up the foil to form 4 parcels and place under a preheated medium broiler for 5–8 minutes, turning once or twice during cooking until the peaches are soft.

Meanwhile, make the sauce. Place the sugar, maple syrup, and butter in a nonstick saucepan over a moderately low heat until the sugar dissolves. Stir continuously until the sauce boils and thickens, which should take about 3 minutes. Add the cream and return to a boil, then immediately remove from the heat.

Drizzle the sauce over the peaches, and serve.

For toffee apples, place 4 halved apples in sheets of foil and divide 1 tablespoon butter between them in cubes, dotting over the top. Sprinkle with a little ground cinnamon and broil for 10–12 minutes until the apples have softened, yet still retain their shape. Serve with the sauce as above.

rainbow tart

Serves **8**
Preparation time **25 minutes**
Cooking time **30 minutes**

12 oz package **sweet pastry**
2 **egg yolks**
3 tablespoons **cornstarch**
3 tablespoons **superfine
  sugar**
⅔ cup **milk**
1 teaspoon **vanilla extract**
1 large **orange**, segmented
1 cup **strawberries**, halved
1 cup **blueberries**
2 thick fresh **pineapple** rings,
  cut into bite-size chunks
2 **kiwifruits**, sliced
confectioners' sugar, to dust
crème fraîche or **plain
  yogurt**, to serve

Line a 9 inch fluted tart pan with the pastry. Trim the edges, then press the pastry firmly into the grooves so the rim sits a little higher than the pan. Fill with scrunched-up nonstick parchment paper and pie weights, then bake in a preheated oven, 350°F, for 15 minutes. Remove the paper and weights and bake for an additional 5 minutes. Set aside to cool.

Mix the egg yolks, cornstarch, and sugar in a bowl. Put the milk in a heavy nonstick pan and bring to a boil. Pour over the egg mixture and blend well using a whisk. Add the vanilla extract, then return to the rinsed-out pan and bring to a boil, beating continuously until boiled and thickened. Transfer to a bowl to cool, stirring occasionally. Cover with plastic wrap to prevent a skin forming.

Place the cooled pastry shell on a serving plate and fill with the custard using a metal spoon to swirl up to the rim. Put the fruit in a bowl and toss to mix, then loosely arrange over the top of the custard. Dust with confectioners' sugar and serve in wedges with spoonfuls of crème fraîche or yogurt.

For sunshine tart, mix 2 segmented oranges, 3 thick slices fresh pineapple, cut into chunks, 2 bananas, cut into chunks and tossed in 2 tablespoons lemon or lime juice, and 1 small mango, cut into chunks. Toss together and use to fill as above.

fairy crumble

Serves **6**

Preparation time **20 minutes**

Cooking time **30 minutes**

3 cups **strawberries**, hulled
and halved

2 cups **raspberries**

1 **orange**, peeled and
segmented

4 tablespoons **superfine
sugar**

½ teaspoon **ground cinnamon**

Topping

2 cups **all-purpose flour**

½ cup **butter**, chilled and
cubed

⅛ cup **brown sugar**

½ cup toasted **hazelnuts**,
roughly chopped, or **slivered
almonds** (optional)

Custard

2 **egg yolks**

2 tablespoons **cornstarch**

3 tablespoons **superfine
sugar**

1½ cups **milk**

2 tablespoons **beet juice**
(from a bought cooked-beet
package) or a drop of
cochineal

Place the strawberries, raspberries, orange segments
(plus any juice), sugar, and cinnamon in a bowl and
toss together gently to coat the fruit lightly in the sugar,
taking care not to break up the raspberries. Transfer
the fruit to a gratin dish and set aside while making the
crumble topping.

Place the flour into a bowl and using your fingertips
blend the butter into it until the mixture resembles fine
bread crumbs. Stir in the sugar and nuts, if using, then
spoon the crumble over the top of the fruit. Bake in
a preheated oven, 400°F, for 25–30 minutes until the
topping is golden and crisp in places.

Make the pink custard: place the egg yolks, cornstarch,
and sugar in a bowl and blend together well. Put the milk
in a heavy nonstick saucepan and bring to a boil. Pour
the milk over the egg mixture, add the beet juice and
beat together well. Return to the heat and cook gently,
stirring continuously until thickened.

Serve the crumble in bowls with the pink custard to
spoon over.

For Caribbean-style crumble, replace the red berries
with 1 large mango, cut into chunks, and 6 thick slices
fresh pineapple, cut into chunks. Toss with the orange
and ½ cup raisins. Replace the nuts with 4 tablespoons
shredded coconut in the crumble. Serve with ice cream
rather than custard.

blueberry & peach pudding

Serves **4**
Preparation time **20 minutes**
Cooking time **40 minutes**

3 **eggs**
1¼ cups **all-purpose flour**
1 cup **confectioners' sugar**,
  plus extra to dust
1¼ cups **milk**
1 teaspoon **vanilla extract**
1 tablespoon **butter**, softened
2 **peaches**, halved, pitted, and
  cut into wedges
1 cup **blueberries**
finely grated zest of 1 **lemon**

Beat the eggs, flour, sugar, milk, and vanilla extract in a bowl until thick and creamy. Heavily grease an 8 inch round pan or ovenproof dish with the butter and arrange the peaches and blueberries inside. Sprinkle with the lemon zest.

Pour the batter over the fruit and bake in a preheated oven, 375°F, for 35 minutes until the batter is firm.

Dust with confectioners' sugar, cut into wedges, and serve warm.

For strawberry, banana, & cherry pudding, replace the peaches and blueberries with 1 large banana, sliced into chunks, 1 cup strawberries, and ½ cup fresh pitted cherries. Try adding 1 teaspoon of ground cinnamon to the fruit and toss if desired.

star-of-the-day dessert

Serves **6**
Preparation time **20 minutes**,
 plus chilling
Cooking time **3 minutes**

¾ cup ready-to-eat **dried
 prunes**, roughly chopped
⅔ cup **water**
4 oz **bittersweet chocolate**
 (70% cocoa solids), broken
 into pieces
2 cups **plain yogurt**
1 oz **milk or semisweet
 chocolate**, made into
 shavings, to decorate

Place the prunes in a pan with the measured water
and bring to a boil. Immediately remove from the
heat, transfer to a food processor, and whiz until
completely smooth.

Return the prunes to the pan with the chocolate
pieces and heat over a very gentle heat, stirring
continuously until the chocolate has melted. Remove
from the heat and beat in the yogurt. Allow to cool.

Divide the dessert between 4 serving glasses and
decorate with the chocolate shavings. Chill for about
30 minutes and serve.

For minted chocolate star-of-the-day dessert, use
a mint-flavored chocolate (70% cocoa solids), dust
the tops with a little organic cocoa powder, and serve
with mint-chocolate sticks for a real treat.

soft-cooked bananas & yogurt ice

Serves **4**

Preparation time **20 minutes**,
  plus freezing

Cooking time **10 minutes**

3 tablespoons **superfine
  sugar**

⅔ cup **water**

4 cups **plain yogurt**

3 teaspoons **vanilla extract**

1 tablespoon **butter**, softened

4 ripe **bananas**

½ teaspoon **ground cinnamon**
  or **nutmeg** (optional)

To serve

4 tablespoons **maple syrup**

½ cup broken **pecan nuts**

Place the sugar and measured water in a heavy saucepan and bring to a boil. Continue to boil for 3–5 minutes until the syrup has reduced by half. Remove from the heat and stir in the yogurt and vanilla extract. Transfer to a freezerproof container and freeze for 3 hours.

Remove the ice from the freezer and beat with a wooden spoon until slushy. Freeze for an additional 4 hours, or overnight, until firm.

Heat the butter in a large nonstick skillet. Halve the bananas lengthwise, then cut each of the halves in half again across its width. Sprinkle the bananas, cut side up, with the spice, if using, and cook in the hot butter for 30–60 seconds on each side until golden. Remove from the pan using a slotted spoon.

Pile the bananas onto serving plates in a lattice pattern, then drizzle with the maple syrup and sprinkle with the pecans. Serve with scoops of the vanilla yogurt ice on top.

For strawberry yogurt ice, to serve as an alternative accompaniment, make as above, replacing the plain yogurt with strawberry yogurt. Cook 2 cups halved strawberries with ½ teaspoon freshly grated orange zest and 1 tablespoon maple syrup in the butter for 2–3 minutes until soft yet retaining their shape. Serve the warm strawberries with the strawberry yogurt ice.

sticky fig & banana traybake

Serves **6**
Preparation time **10 minutes**
Cooking time **20 minutes**

½ cup **margarine** or **butter**, softened
½ cup **brown sugar**
1 teaspoon **ground ginger**
2 **eggs**
1 cup **all-purpose flour**
3 **figs**, quartered
1 large **banana**, cut into chunks
2 tablespoons **maple syrup**
ice cream or **vanilla custard**, to serve

Beat the margarine or butter and sugar until smooth and creamy. Add the ginger, eggs, and flour and beat again until a smooth mixture is formed. Lightly grease a 9 inch square pan or ovenproof dish, then spoon in the mixture and level with the back of a spoon.

Toss the figs and banana with the maple syrup and arrange over the top of the cake, pressing the fruit into the cake in places. Bake in a preheated oven, 350°F, for 20 minutes until the cake is well risen and golden and the fruit is soft.

Serve the cake in squares with either scoops of ice cream or vanilla custard (see below).

For vanilla custard to serve as an accompaniment, heat 1¼ cups milk, with the seeds of ½ vanilla bean scraped into it, in a nonstick pan until boiling. Meanwhile, blend 2 egg yolks with 1 teaspoon cornstarch and 2 tablespoons superfine sugar. Pour the milk over the egg mixture once boiled and beat well to blend. Return to the heat, stirring continuously until just beginning to boil and thicken. It will coat the back of a spoon.

end-of-summer custard pie

Serves **6–8**

Preparation time **20 minutes**, plus chilling

Cooking time **25 minutes**

1¼ cups **all-purpose flour**, plus extra for dusting

3 tablespoons **custard powder**

2 tablespoons **confectioners' sugar**

⅓ cup **butter**, chilled and cut into cubes

2–3 tablespoons **cold water**

3 cups **blackberries**

2 **apples**, peeled, cored, and roughly chopped

4 tablespoons **superfine sugar**

1 tablespoon **honey**

beaten **egg**

vanilla ice cream (optional) or **crème fraîche** (optional), to serve

Sift the flour, custard powder, and confectioners' sugar into a bowl. Blend the butter using your fingertips into the flour until the mixture resembles fine bread crumbs. Sprinkle over the measured water, then using a round-bladed knife begin to work the mixture into a smooth, firm dough. Wrap and chill for 15 minutes.

Toss the blackberries and apples with the sugar and honey and place in an 8 inch round pie dish or ovenproof dish.

Roll out the pastry, on a well-floured surface, to a round slightly larger than the pie dish. Place the dish on the pastry and cut around it using a sharp knife to produce a circle the correct size for the top. Using the pastry trimmings, make a border strip about ½ inch wide. Dampen the edges of the pie dish and fit the strips of pastry around the edge, pressing firmly. Dampen this pastry too before placing the circle on top and pressing again firmly to hold in place. Using any remaining trimmings, decorate the pie with leaves, flowers, birds, or other shapes.

Brush with beaten egg to glaze and bake in a preheated oven, 400°F, for 20–25 minutes until golden and crisp. Serve with vanilla ice cream or crème fraîche, if desired.

For cinnamon & peach custard pie, drain 2 x 13 oz cans of peaches in natural juice and toss with the apples, 1 tablespoon brown sugar, and 1 teaspoon ground cinnamon. Use instead of the blackberries with the custard pastry as above.

spider's web pancakes

Serves **8**
Preparation time **15 minutes**
Cooking time **15–20 minutes**

2 **eggs**
1¼ cups **all-purpose flour**
1 teaspoon **superfine sugar**
1¼ cups **milk**
1 tablespoon **butter**, melted
1¼ cups **heavy cream**
3 teaspoons **honey**
2 cups **raspberries**
vegetable oil, for frying
confectioners' sugar, to dust

Beat the eggs, flour, and sugar in a bowl until well combined, then beat in the milk until you have a smooth batter. Beat in the melted butter, then set the batter aside.

Whip the cream very lightly until just beginning to peak, then fold in the honey and raspberries and chill while making the pancakes.

Heat a few drops of oil in a small, nonstick skillet. Transfer the batter to a pitcher with a narrow spout, and pour a very thin stream of the batter, starting in the center of the pan and continuing in continuous circles around, then across the pan to form a small web pattern about 6 inches in diameter. Cook for about 1 minute until set, then, using a spatula, flip the pancake over and cook the other side for 30 seconds. Repeat to make 8 pancakes, stacking them between sheets of nonstick parchment paper to keep warm.

Serve the warm pancakes filled with a little raspberry cream and dusted with confectioners' sugar.

For apple & cinnamon spider's web pancakes,
place 2 large peeled, cored, and roughly chopped cooking apples in a pan with 3 tablespoons golden raisins, 3 tablespoons water, ½ teaspoon ground cinnamon, and 2 tablespoons brown sugar. Cook over a gentle heat for 3–5 minutes, stirring continuously until soft and pulpy. Remove from the heat and allow to cool. Serve folded into the cream as above, replacing the raspberries, or fill the pancakes with the apple mixture alone and serve with yogurt.

no-sugar brownies with berries

Serves **12**
Preparation time **20 minutes**
Cooking time **30 minutes**

8 oz **bittersweet chocolate**
  (70% cocoa solids)
½ cup **unsalted butter**
4 **eggs**
1¼ cups **all-purpose flour**
½ cup **ground almonds**
½ cup **semisweet chocolate
  chips**
½ cup **pecan nuts**, roughly
  chopped (optional)

To serve
fresh **blueberries, raspberries,
  and strawberries**
ice cream or **crème fraîche**

Lightly grease an 11 x 7 inch baking pan and line the base with nonstick parchment paper.

Melt the chocolate together with the butter (see page 180). Remove from the heat and allow to cool for 2 minutes. Beat the eggs in a separate bowl until frothy (about 3 minutes), then stir in the cooled chocolate mixture.

Fold in the flour, ground almonds, chocolate chips, and pecans, if using. Transfer to the prepared baking pan and bake in a preheated oven, 350°F, for 25–30 minutes until just firm to the touch.

Allow the brownies to cool in the pan for 20 minutes before cutting into 12 squares and serving with the fresh berries and ice cream or crème fraîche.

For white chocolate & strawberry brownies

(containing sugar in the chocolate), replace the bittersweet chocolate with white chocolate, and the chocolate chips and pecans with ¾ cup strawberries, finely chopped. This brownie will be soft and will only keep in the refrigerator for 3 days.

fruity refreshers

fresh lemonade

Makes **7½ cups**
Preparation time **4–5 minutes**,
   plus cooling
Cooking time **4–5 minutes**

⅓ cup **superfine sugar**
7½ cups **water**
4 **lemons**, sliced, plus extra
   slices to serve
ice cubes

Place the sugar in a pan with 2½ cups of the measured water and all the sliced lemons. Bring to a boil, stirring well until all the sugar has dissolved.

Remove from the heat and add all the remaining water. Stir, then set aside to cool completely.

Once cold, roughly crush the lemons, to release all the juice. Strain through a sieve, add the ice cubes, and serve in glasses decorated with slices of lemon.

For fresh limeade, simply use 6 limes instead of 4 lemons, or use a mixture of the two. Try adding chopped mint while the limeade cools for a refreshing mint flavor. Strain as above.

mango, melon, & orange juice

Makes 1¾ **cups**
Preparation time **5–6 minutes**

1 ripe **mango**, roughly
 chopped
½ **Galia melon**, seeded and
 roughly chopped
¾ cup **orange juice**
2 **ice cubes**

Place the mango and melon in a blender and whiz until smooth.

Add the orange juice and ice cubes, then puree until smooth. Serve immediately.

For coconut & pineapple juice, place 1 x 13 oz can coconut milk in a food processor with ½ small pineapple, peeled, cored, and roughly chopped. Whiz until smooth, then serve poured over ice and decorated with fresh cherries or strawberries for color.

strawberry & vanilla milkshake

Serves **2**
Preparation time **5–6 minutes**,
   plus cooling
Cooking time **5–6 minutes**

1¼ cups **milk**
1¼ cups **light cream**
½ **vanilla bean**
1½ cups **strawberries**, hulled

Put the milk and cream in a pan. Remove the vanilla seeds from the bean using the back of a teaspoon and place the pod and seeds in the pan with the milk and cream. Bring to a boil, stirring. Once boiling point has been reached, remove from the heat and allow to cool completely.

Place the strawberries in a food processor and whiz until smooth. Add the cooled vanilla milk and whiz again until pink. Pour into chilled glasses and serve with straws.

For strawberry & vanilla ice cream milkshake, put the milk and strawberries in a food processor with 5 scoops of good-quality vanilla ice cream (the variety with vanilla seeds within the ice cream) and whiz until smooth and blended. Add some ice and whiz again. Pour into chilled glasses and serve.

watermelon & raspberry juice

Makes **about ¾ cup**
Preparation time **5–6 minutes**

10 oz **watermelon**
   (¼ an average fruit), seeded
   and chopped
1 cup **raspberries**
ice cubes, crushed (optional)

Put the watermelon and raspberries in a blender and whiz until smooth. Press the juice through a sieve to remove any raspberry seeds.

Pour the juice into glasses over some crushed ice cubes, if desired.

For melon & apple juice, place half a small, seeded and chopped, green melon into a food processor with 1 green apple, cored and cut into wedges (keep the skin on). Add 1 tablespoon lemon juice and whiz until smooth. Pour over crushed ice if desired.

nectarine & raspberry yogurt ice

Serves **2**
Preparation time **5 minutes**

3 ripe **nectarines**, halved
  and pitted
1½ cups **raspberries**
⅔ cup **plain yogurt**
handful of **ice cubes**

Put the nectarines and raspberries in a food processor and whiz until really smooth. Add the yogurt and whiz again, then add the ice and whiz until very crushed and the shake thickens.

Pour into chilled glasses. Decorate with cocktail umbrellas and anything else to make the drink look fun!

For banana & mango coconut ice, replace the nectarines and raspberries with 1 large ripe banana and 1 mango, cut into chunks, and whiz until smooth. Add ⅔ cup coconut milk and whiz again. Add the ice and whiz until the shake thickens. Pour into chilled glasses to serve.

fruity popsicles

Makes **4**

Preparation time **7–8 minutes**, plus freezing

2 **peaches**, peeled, pitted, and cut into chunks
1¼ cups **water**
1 **red apple**, peeled
¾ cup **strawberries**, hulled

Place the peaches in a blender and whiz until smooth. Add one-third of the measured water and divide evenly between 4 popsicle molds. Freeze until just set.

Chop the apples into even-size chunks and juice them. Add one-third of the water and pour on top of the frozen peach mixture, then freeze until just set.

Hull the strawberries and juice them. Add the remainder of the water and pour on top of the frozen apple mixture, then freeze until set.

For chocolate & orange popsicles, place 1 x 10 oz can mandarin segments in a food processor and whiz until smooth. Place into a pan with 4 oz organic 70 per cent cocoa solids bittersweet chocolate and gently heat until the chocolate has melted. Stir well with the orange puree and pour into 4 popsicle molds. Freeze for 2 hours until firm.

traffic-light smoothie

Makes 1¾ **cups**
Preparation time **9–10 minutes**

3 **kiwifruits**, roughly chopped
⅔ cup **tangy-flavored yogurt**
   (such as lemon or orange)
1 small **mango**, roughly
   chopped
2 tablespoons **orange** or
   apple juice
1¼ cups **raspberries**
1–2 teaspoons **honey**

Whiz the kiwifruits in a blender until smooth and spoon the mixture into 2 tall glasses. Top each with a spoonful of yogurt, spreading the yogurt to the sides of the glasses.

Blend the mango to a puree with the orange or apple juice and spoon into the glasses. Top with another layer of yogurt.

Whiz the raspberries and push through a sieve over a bowl to extract the seeds. Check their sweetness (you might need to stir in a little honey if they are very sharp). Spoon the raspberry puree into glasses to serve.

For zebra layered blackberry smoothie, place 1 cup blackberries into a food processor with 2 tablespoons honey and whiz until smooth. Layer alternately with the yogurt to replace the kiwi, mango, and orange juice.

index

acknowledgments

Author's acknowledgments

Thank you to my sister Sophie for all her help and support during the writing of this book. Also a big thank you to Sophie's and my children for being the tried and trusted recipe testers!

Executive Editor Nicky Hill
Editor Kerenza Swift
Executive Art Editor Mark Stevens
Designer Richard Scott
Photographer Lis Parsons
Home Economist Emma Jane Frost
Props Stylist Liz Hippisley
Production Controller Carolin Stransky

Commissioned photography © Octopus Publishing
Group Ltd/Lis Parsons apart from the following:
© Octopus Publishing Group Limited/Vanessa Davies
8, 11, 12, 115, 158, 163, 169, 185, 191, 193, 225,
228, 233, 235.